ROCK 'N' ROLL AND FAST CARS

PHOTOGRAPHS BY MARTYN GODDARD

Published in 2016 by Really Useful Products Ltd

1st Edition

ISBN 978-1-5262-0521-6

All rights reserved. No part of this book
may be reproduced, stored in a retrieval system,
or transmitted in any form or by any means, electronic,
electrostatic, magnetic tape, mechanical, photocopying, recording
or otherwise without permission in writing from the publishers.

All information correct at time of original publishing. The publisher
cannot be responsible for the veracity of any information contained
within this edition.

© All images Copyright of Martyn Goddard
© All words Copyright of Martyn Goddard, Dale Drinnon,
Car magazine and Automobile magazine

Designed by Tilley Associates
tilleyassociates.com

Print production by Cousin
cousin.uk.com

Pre-media production by Pavement
pavement.uk.com

Printed and bound in England

MIKE PICKLES, entrepreneur
and kind sponsor of this book.

MIKE PICKLES

I've not known Martyn for so long but I have known and loved his work going all the way back to The Jam. I loved the images but had no idea or interest really in who took them. Fast forward and about a year ago a friend of mine was working on a photo shoot and told me the photographer was quite a character – I now know this remark was an understatement. We met a week or so later in Lake Como at a car event and as I was driving an interesting car Martyn suggested that he took an image. As I am always relaxed I agreed and then we had a long long discussion on our joint love of music and cars. If I was to summarise Martyn I would say he never shuts up. This is rich coming from me.

We discovered we were both separately invited to The Jam exhibition a month later at Somerset House curated by Nicky Weller. It turned out we were both also on the list of thanks. Nicky had also told Martyn that I helped support her book Growing up with The Jam.

A while later Martyn out of the blue made the trek up north to see me and asked for support on this venture. I was keen to see his previous work and Martyn knew that my reaction was key to support. He nervously handed over his other books and I was blown away by the composition, emotion and use of colour. I immediately said yes and – a few months later – here is the book. I hope you enjoy the book as much as me.

Mike Pickles, June 2016.

NICK MASON, in his garage
in Kings Cross, London with his
1962 Ferrari GTO, 1990s.

NICK MASON

Our paths first crossed in the early 1980s when Martyn was assigned to photograph not the members of our band, but my Maserati Birdcage for Supercar Classics magazine. He dropped in to show me the prints, which were of course terrific, and fortuitously I was looking for someone to take some really good pictures of some of my cars.

The fact that he lived locally was an added bonus, as he was familiar with the Kings Cross landscapes and backdrops. The combination of a disused school opposite our workshop, and the occasional trip to Camden Town to use the railway arch at the bottom of Martyn's street provided everything he needed.

Over the years there's been a lot of film exposed. Everything from the D Type Jaguar for Classic Cars, to a marathon day's shooting of my model car collection for a Japanese magazine.

When he's not wallowing in a multi-decibel mosh pit I've found Martyn snapping me in the pit lane at Goodwood, the paddock of a VSCC meeting at Silverstone and he even turned up at a collectors car restoration symposium in Florida with camera at the ready.

This book showcases a small selection of images Martyn has produced over a long and varied career. He's known for his photographs of some of the most iconic characters in the music industry, but equally for his images of some of the equally important automobiles. In my view it's not a bad combination!

Nick Mason, June 2016.

SIR PAUL SMITH, photographed
in his office in Covent Garden,
London, May 2013.

SIR PAUL SMITH

Fast cars and rock'n'roll have always gone hand in hand. As someone that has worked with many musicians and photographed many cars, Martyn's very well-placed to put this book together, it's great for anyone who loves rock'n'roll and fast cars!

Paul Smith, July 2016.

BILL SMITH, art director of album
covers for The Jam and The Cure,
photographed in my studio, May 1977.

BILL SMITH

Martyn and I started working together in March 1977. I was art director at Polydor Records and in 1976 The Jam were signed to Polydor through Chris Parry. I was incredibly excited about working with Paul and the gang; having worked my way through the Polydor roster in the previous 18 months, here was a band just starting on the road to stardom and a chance to really create a new visual force.

As an art director you need to work with like-minded photographers and illustrators, who get where you're coming from and what you want to achieve with covers. Martyn was exactly the right man for the job on In The City, the first album and singles for shoot for The Jam. We tried to create an idea that the guys were in an underground toilet, as if they'd escaped there having been chased by persons unknown. I wanted this shot to be in graphic black and white and look like it might appear in the press. We couldn't do this for 'real' so we had to create the situation in a studio. Martyn is meticulous in his preparation for each shoot with lighting, set designs and artist placements within the set. So we ended up building a back wall and then together tiling this backdrop. When the band arrived we took a couple of quick Polaroids based on Martyn's set-ups, I moved the band away and sprayed The Jam logo (a case of we 'wos' here) and then lined the band against the wall. One roll of film later we had it! Martyn doesn't like to waste film and I don't like to waste time.

Martyn has always been terrific to work with and after the first Jam session we worked on many, many album and single covers together very successfully in my opinion – in a strange way we complimented each other in our working styles. His work then and now is testament to his vigilant eye for detail and meticulous preparations. Too many people think photography is just clicking the shutter and hoping for the best; Martyn belies this notion, which is why he is still working all these years later.

Bill Smith, May 2016.

"Blondie in Camera"
14 8 78 DH

**DEBBIE HARRY AND
MARTYN GODDARD,**
Polaroid photograph by Chris Stein,
New York, May 1978.

ABOUT THIS BOOK

In 2007 I staged an exhibition at the Exposure Gallery London to mark the 30th anniversary of the release of The Jam In the City album, which I had shot in 1977. Since graduating from Harrow College of Technology & Art in the early 1970s I had found myself working for various rock bands including groups in the new wave and punk genre, and it was also around that time that I undertook automotive assignments for Car magazine. For the exhibition I assembled a group of prints of Rock & Roll artists and supercars that I had photographed. I hope the visitors thought it an interesting mix of images representing people and machines of the era.

Now ten years later and after the publication of a book on road trips around France titled 'An Omelette & Three Glasses of Wine' I have, with the help of Mike Pickles, produced this book of photographs covering forty-plus years working as a photographer. I have always been a freelancer, which has given me freedom to work for an array of interesting magazines and record labels. It's been an extension of my teenage dreams of music and fast cars that my chosen profession has given me the ability to be a part of, as I can't play a note of music and only managed fourth place in my ten-year career as a historic rally driver. The book is all about the images, the people and automobiles. Browsing the pages of photographs and reading accompanying copy and reprints of period stories, I hope you will be able to appreciate some great artists, automobiles and events that I was on hand to record in my own way. Over the 150 pages, with the help of editor David Lillywhite, it illustrates the enjoyment I have had working on the assignments. Not all went as planned but all shoots were fun on reflection!

I started my career as a dyslexic photographer but due to the massive changes in the technology and the publishing business I am now a photojournalist, producing words to accompany the images. In the early days, I presented my portfolio to magazines and record companies, picture editors and art directors and it was a couple of these who gave me the career breaks such as the Queen live gig in 1975 and my first Car magazine assignment, which turned out to be photographing a Bedford show truck. Today my images are marketed via the internet; efficient but I miss the personal contact. Nowadays, from time to time I lecture to student photographers, by chance at my old college, now called Westminster University. My opening comment is something like, "the only thing that is the same today as that day in 1973 when I graduated is that light passes through the lens of a camera".

Today we are bombarded by imagery via social media, most of a throwaway nature, around a trillion taken in 2015 alone. I continue using the latest digital cameras, processing the images on my computer giving me greater control, the holy grail of every photographer, which was only dreamt of in the classic film stock era. Enzo Ferrari was often asked which was his favourite Ferrari; he replied his marque's next automobile. I have my favourite photographs but still delight in producing new images in new ways. As they say, you are only as good as your last assignment!

George Weidenfeld and Nicolson Limited

Weidenfeld & Nicolson

Registered Office 91 Clapham High Street, London SW4 7TA   *Telephone* 01-622 9933

Registered number 472173 England   *Telegrams and cables* Nicobar London SW4 7TA   *Telex* 918066

27 July 1982

John Stonehouse
Litagency

Dear John Stonehouse

I am replying to your letter of 12th July addressed to
Lord Weidenfeld.

I am not sure that I have seen the work of Martyn Goddard
but I am afraid that I do not see much international
appeal in a book featuring photographic portraits of
people such as Shirley Conran and Terry Wogan.

To be frank, I do not believe that anyone buys a book
of portraits because they are interested in the personalities
but rather that they are perhaps the cream of the work of an
eminent photographer - Bill Brandt and Arnold Newman for
example. The only exceptions that I see working are those
where there is a coherent theme in the book; we are, for
instance, publishing a UK edition of an American book
featuring one photographer's portraits of opera stars,
since this has an undoubted appeal to opera lovers. Since
there is no evident theme in Mr Goddard's work, nor with
respect is he a photographer whose name is widely known, I
really do not believe that this is something for us.

Yours sincerely

RUSSELL ASH

WEIDENFELD & NICHOLSON,
letter of rejection, July 1982.

CONTENTS

ROCK 'N' ROLL

FAST CARS

ROCK 'N' ROLL

1975 – 1994

QUEEN LIVE

1974 – 1977

FREDDIE MERCURY, on stage at
Hyde Park, London, 1977.

Left: **FREDDIE MERCURY,** Prism lens image shot at Hammersmith Odeon, 1975. This page: **FREDDIE MERCURY,** in the spotlight playing grand piano Southampton, May 1977.

QUEEN

My introduction to Queen came in 1975 via the PR at Elton John's Rocket Records. Elton's manager John Reid had recently taken over the management of Queen, who had by this time become stratospheric. I had a good portfolio of images of the band playing live at Hammersmith Odeon in 1974, which Disc magazine had run as a cover story, so the management assigned me to photograph the band's Hyde Park and Cardiff Castle gigs. They all went well despite torrential rail in the Welsh capital! Being the management's photographer didn't help with personal contact as on every photo shoot I did with the band I never managed to talk to them.

On one memorable video shoot in Surrey on a hot summer's day, the group were being filmed playing in a the barn lit by thousands of candles. I was granted a few minutes to grab some production stills on set on the promise of a proper shoot after the video wrap. Needless to say, after hours of location catering and reading the papers the band disappeared for the last time as far as I was concerned!

Left: **FREDDIE MERCURY,** on stage
Hammersmith Odeon, 1975. This
page: **FREDDIE MERCURY,** on stage
in Southampton, 1977.

This page: **BRIAN MAY,** Hyde Park, London, 1976. Right: **ROGER TAYLOR,** Cardiff Castle, 1976.

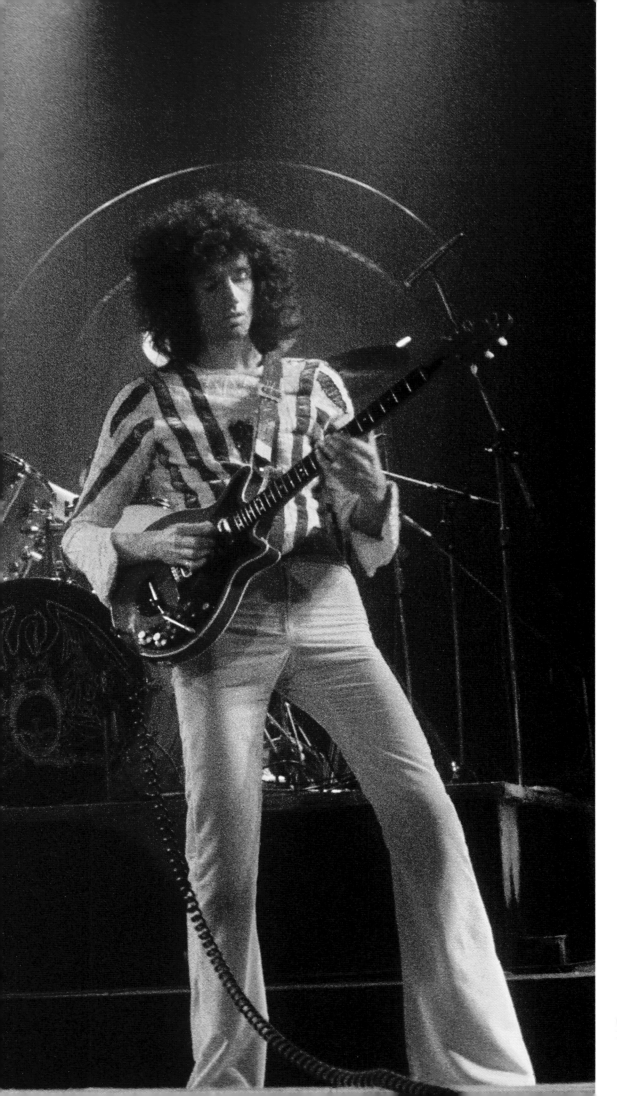

FREDDIE MERCURY & BRIAN MAY,
Hammersmith Odeon, May 1975.

PUNK AND NEW WAVE

1977 – 1980

DEBBIE HARRY OF BLONDIE,
live at The Palladium New York, 1978.

THE JAM

I had a phone call from Bill Smith, one of the art directors at Polydor Records, in late February 1977. He had to produce an LP cover for a new band, which he was excited about but as usual it was an urgent assignment as the record company wanted to release the album in May. The New Wave band was named The Jam, a three-piece outfit comprising of Bruce Foxton, Rick Buckler and Paul Weller, who to quote Bill "is a bloke with definite ideas about the group's image". At this point I hadn't met any member of the band or seen a photograph. Bill's concept for the cover was to photograph the group in an urban location featuring a wall of white tiles with graffiti sprayed logo, as the album title was 'In The City'. I thought of all the problems a location shoot would incur because of the need to spray paint on a wall and the permissions and permits that would be required. The shoot would also take time, as we needed to produce front, back and inner sleeve images. It was decided to shoot in my studio in Kensington Church Street using a couple of 8' x 4' flats tiled in 4 inch white Crystal tiles. I can't remember whether it was budget or time constraints but Bill and I tiled the flats the morning of the session, 2nd March 1977, and it was Bill who took the black spray paint and in one attempt produced the iconic logo on the white ceramic tiles as the glue was setting.

The band arrived at my cramped studio wearing mod suits and carrying Rickenbacker guitars. Bruce's bass was a copy at this time and Rick brought a snare drum. I have since learned that the band had to scramble the clothes together in the mad rush to release the record and the old trainers worn that day were replaced in later shoots by two-toned leather loafers. We didn't hang around after the hairdresser had trimmed their hair; we were all ready to shoot. Looking at my original photo journal, I used two large studio flashlights with metal reflectors either side and close to the lens of my Hasselblad 500CM camera to produce a fashion style shadowless effect. I shot Polaroid test prints, which only needed minor adjustments before clipping a black and white film back on the camera and shooting two rolls of the film that was to become the front cover.

There is always a tension on a shoot with a new band and so once Bill and myself felt we had the shot, shooting extra film stock would have compromised the rest of the shoot. For the back cover we shot individual images in colour and black and white of each band member with their own instrument. Both guitarists had no problem moving while playing an acoustic set while I snapped away. When it came to Rick and his drums, or the one drum he had brought along, it was more difficult so we settled for the drummer leaning on the wall shading his eyes from the bright lights. The individual shots completed, it was lunch – always a highlight of any shoot – with sandwiches from the local dairy, and then it was bye to the band.

Bill and I then set about photographing the wall in various stages of distress, Bill smashing tiles and spraying new words. I photographed the vandalism of the wall of tiles, which were used as the back cover, record label and inner sleeve note sheet on the finished LP. The Jam's first album 'In the City' released on May 20th 1977, reached 20 in the UK album chart and has been produced in 51 versions over the years. Following that first photo session I worked on seven projects with the band producing press, promotion and record covers.

This page: **BRUCE FOXTON AND RICK BUCKLER OF THE JAM,** 'In the City' studio session Kensington, London, May 1977. Right: **PAUL WELLER AND THE JAM,** 'In the City' studio session Kensington, London, May 1977.

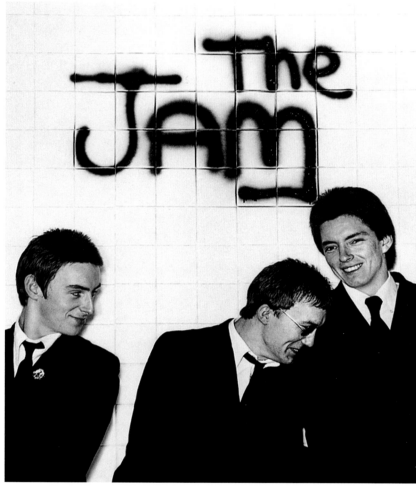

In an era of picture single record covers, a combination of Weller, Smith and Goddard produced a series of releases over the next two years based on the Soho district in the West End of London. Many of the band's titles echoed this location, which in the swinging sixties had been central to the Mod culture of fashion and music such as the Mary Quant, Lord John and John Stevens boutiques and with the bands, Small Faces, The Who and Rolling Stones playing at the 100 Club and The Marquee. In July 1977, Bruce Foxton even titled a B-side 'Carnaby Street'.

For the cover 'News of the World', the band wanted to continue the Carnaby Street theme so we met up in Soho early on a cold damp winter's day. The plan was to shoot the group walking down the street towards the viewer as if you were passing them in the street. The dull weather wasn't such a problem as Westminster Council had pedestrianised the street, covering the road surface with yellow, black and orange rubber flooring, and the early start meant that there was just the odd fashion store assistant scurrying to work. Looking at the image now I get the sense of the band split into two parts, Paul Weller on his own on the left and Butler and Foxton apart on the right. The shoot was necessarily short due to the busy location and the group members complaining at the early start and lack of breakfast.

As luck would have it I knew the Soho area well, not because I frequented the many dodgy strip clubs and bars in the area but because my father-in-law ran an electrical contracting business in adjacent Beak Street and he was the fount of all knowledge when it came to local cafés. I led the way to Frank's Café around the corner where I shot one of the most informal and interesting rolls of 35mm film of the band, and once again slightly separated Paul Weller on the left having a cup of tea and smoke while the rhythm section tucked into a good fry up!

Most of the six other photo shoots for The Jam were studio sessions in Church Street, Kensington. Bill would phone a few days before the shoot and I would make sure that I had the backgrounds and lighting equipment ready, such as the mirror used for the image on the cover of 'Growing Up with The Jam' book. My method of working at that time was to try and make the session quick and interesting as the young musicians had a short boredom threshold. It was up to myself and the art director to know what we wanted to produce and then get on with it. With New Wave bands, shoots rarely took all day.

The Jam 'All around the World' single cover, shot in May 1977, was the first planned colour photo session; the band again wearing their signature black mod suits but now with stylish two-tone loafer shoes. The plan was to keep the cover simple; it was a full-length band shot with a bright yellow background for dramatic effect, using fashion photography lighting. The record made 13 in the UK record charts.

THE JAM, Frank's café Lexington Street. After ' News Of the World' record cover shoot, 1978.

THE JAM, on Bond Street tube
station for Down in the Tube Station
at Midnight photo shoot, 1977.

"WE CHOSE BOND
STREET TUBE STATION
ON THE CENTRAL LINE,
I THINK BECAUSE BILL
SMITH KNEW THE
STATION WELL FROM
HIS DAILY COMMUTE."

MARTYN GODDARD

In September 1978 for the 'Down in the Tube Station at Midnight' single cover it was decided to shoot on location. We chose Bond Street tube station on the Central line, I think because Bill Smith knew the station well from his daily commute. We waited to late evening before our raid on the station as this was going to be a quick shoot i.e. we didn't have permission. I used a 35mm Nikon camera with fast b/w film pushed to the limit to take the photographs without a tripod, hence the resulting grainy images. The band pitched themselves at the end of the platform and I waited until a speeding train emerged out of the tunnel before pressing the shutter! We only shot with about five trains before making an exit to street level.

Another location cover was 'Strange Town'; this was an unusual cover to shoot. Bill Smith described the image he was looking for, a crossroads with a signpost and a lone figure in the centre of the road – "and by the way it will be all soft focus". I had a think and remembered a road junction in the fields on the Isle of Thanet in Kent close to the village of Acol. The band were not involved in the shoot so Bill and I drove down from London. Bill was the model as the image was deliberately out of focus and the photograph was representing am atmosphere rather than an actual location! The record got to 15 in the UK Top Twenty.

My last assignment didn't involve working with the group. Bill Smith asked me to shoot various still life and street scene images for the 'Sound Affects' album in July 1980. It was an interesting assignment walking around Camden Town to find the right shots. One I remember was a funeral procession in York Way and another involved calling up friends and family to find models, a baby and a jukebox for the eclectic images required by the brief. The LP was released in November 1980.

IAN DURY

I first photographed Ian Dury at the Victoria Palace when his band Kilburn and the High Roaders were the support act for Shanana in 1974. He was a charismatic front man even if the rest of the band were a bit wayward. Six years later the Telegraph Sunday magazine asked me to shoot a profile of Ian Dury, who was now top of the pops.

Our first session was in Putney where I met the PR from Stiff Records, Magenta Divine, who was nothing if not stylish. It started to rain and things looked bleak until Ian arrived in a green Ford Cortina and shouted, "Where do you want to take the snaps?" or words to that effect! The rain was heavy by now but deep in the boot of my car I had an old golf umbrella that was colourful and large. It saved the day and we walked along the River Thames shooting at will and producing an interesting set of images to start the profile.

Home shoots were popular with the magazine editor but not with Ian Dury so my next set of images were taken at a studio recording session in deepest Harlesden. Being keen, I turned up on time and on arrival two things were made clear; no flash photography and of course Ian hadn't arrived yet. The place was dimly lit with fluorescent tubes and the odd spotlight so any hope of colour photography was out. I chose my good old stand by, black and white Tri X film rated at 800 ASA, which would produce documentary style grainy prints. I settled down reading old copies of NME and studio recording trade magazines for a while until my subject turned up. A quick hello, then into the studio until early afternoon and yes, we could shoot while the band took a break.

IAN DURY, photographed in his Ford
Cortina in Putney, London, 1980.

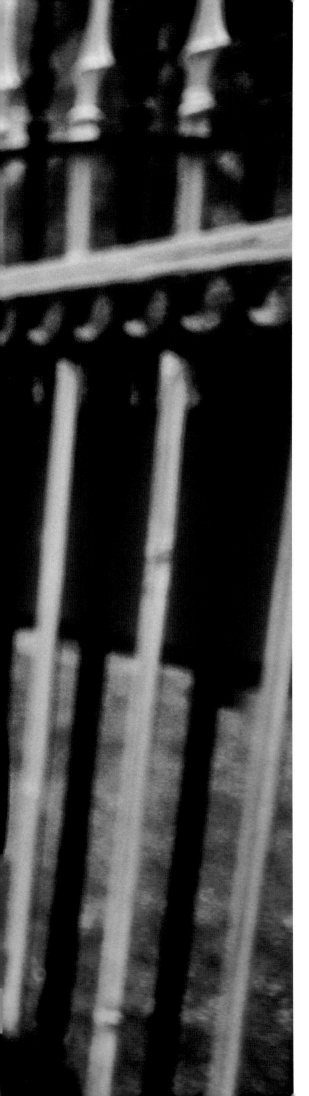

DEBBIE HARRY, walking in
the street next to Gramercy
Park New York, May 1978.

PUNK AND NEW WAVE

BLONDIE

In late June 1978 I found myself in the Record Plant studios in New York City with Blondie. They were in the studio recording their third album Parallel Lines. This was my second visit to photograph the band as a month earlier I had taken a £99 Freddie Laker DC10 flight to spend a week with them, staying in the Gramercy Park hotel shooting Debbie Harry. This became a cover story for the Telegraph Sunday magazine. I had travelled with the group to Philadelphia when they were the support band for Alice Cooper and enjoyed photographing the band's one-off gig at the Palladium in New York.

So when I arrived at the studio for the first photo session for record company Chrysalis, one of several planned for the week, I could sense a tense atmosphere. As a photographer, shooting in recording studios was always a problem on a technical level with period camera equipment and film stock, in what were very dark functional spaces. Additionally, one had to work around the process of recording a record. It was soon evident that Blondie and Debbie Harry in particular were having issues with record producer Mike Chapman. The band's New York Punk heritage clashed with Chapman's quest for West Coast-style perfection. While I shot the images on contact sheet R427E (the negatives now lost), Debbie would have to sing short vocal passages, which were over dubbed time after time, hence the various facial expressions she was making to the camera! Stiflingly boring in production for all members of the band, the album was to take just six weeks to record. Despite the record company's doubts about the album, it produced hit singles and reached number 6 in the US Billboard chart and number 1 in the UK album chart. The rest is history.

This page: **DEBBIE HARRY,** photo shoot at the Gramercy Park Hotel, New York, for Telegraph Sunday magazine, May 1978. Right: **DEBBIE HARRY,** at Record Plant Studio, New York, recording Parallel Lines album, 1978.

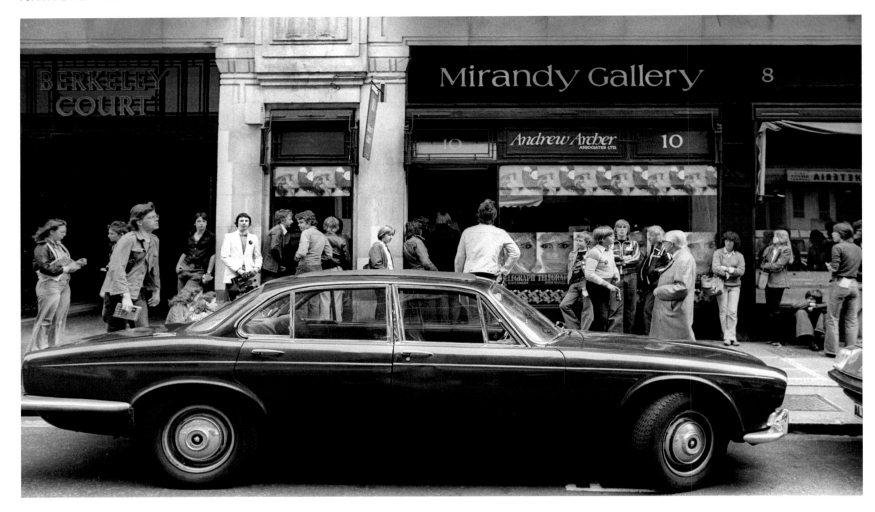

This page: **BLONDIE FANS,** photographs of Blondie fans outside my photo exhibition at The Mirandy Gallery in London, August 1978.
Right: **DEBBIE HARRY,** Debbie Harry leaning on my tripod with my Nikon FE camera. Photo shoot on New York rooftop, 1978.

In August 1978, in association with Chrysalis Records and the Telegraph Sunday magazine, I staged the exhibition 'Blondie in Camera' at The Mirandy Gallery in Glentworth Street, London. It was a collection of the images from the two shoots in New York that year. The exhibition opening was to be the media launch of the latest single 'Picture This' and the presentation of a silver disc for 'Plastic Letter' album, so at 2.30pm 14th August the band arrived, making their way through the crowded street full of fans who had been waiting all that morning. I certainly enjoyed the event, which was given serious media coverage and we were able to sell signed prints for the band's favourite charity supporting diabetes research. I still have three prints but over the two weeks of the exhibition, three life size cut outs of Debbie Harry and the white label 'kissed' LP that I used for the Parallel Lines picture disc shot all went AWOL!

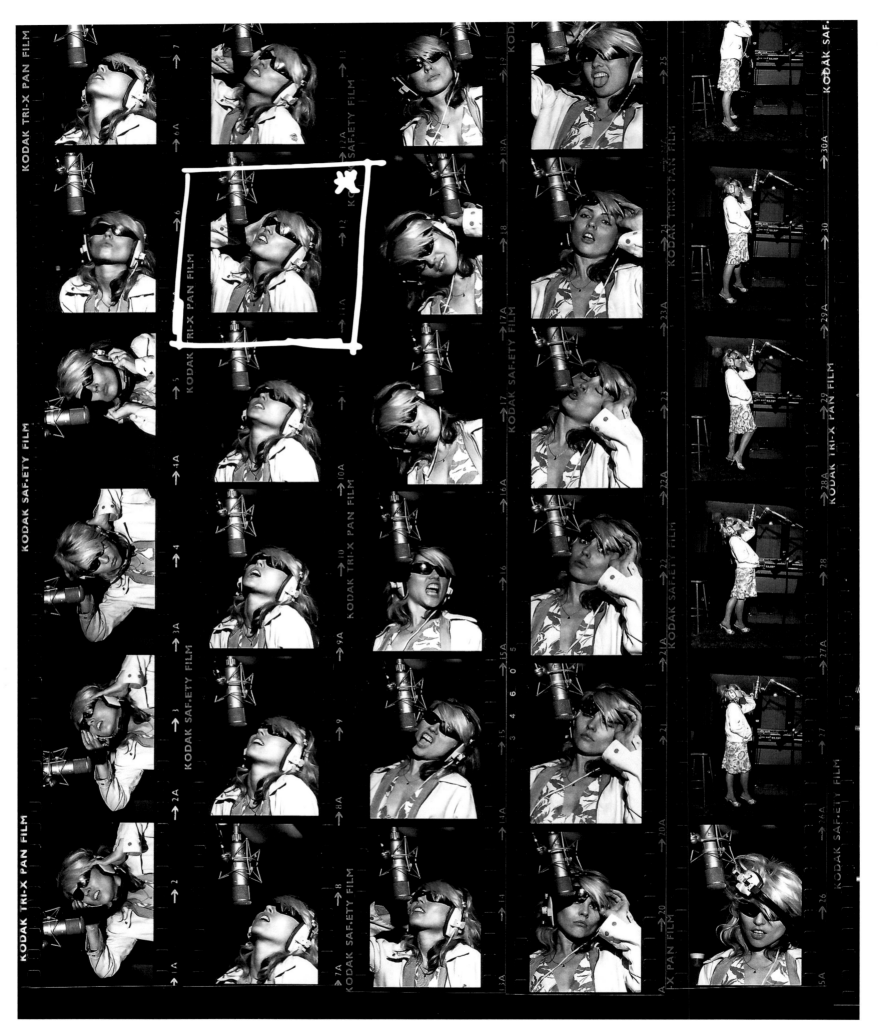

Left: **DEBBIE HARRY,** contact sheet from
photo shoot with Debbie at Record Plant Studio
New York recording Parallel Lines album, 1978.
This page: **DEBBIE HARRY,** photo shoot for
Telegraph Sunday magazine used on Parallel
Lines picture disc. New York, 1978.

DEBBIE HARRY, on the
Blondie Tour bus on route
to Philadelphia, 1978.

This page: **DEBBIE HARRY & CHRIS
STEIN,** photographed on Lexington
St New York, 1978. Right: **DEBBIE
HARRY,** opening party of 'Blondie in
camera' exhibition Mirandy Gallery
London, August 1978.

POP AND PROG

1974 – 1992

GENESIS, Olympic Stadium,
Munich, Germany. Photo shoot for
Three sides live album shoot, 1982

Left: **AC/DC,** contact sheet from the first shoot in the UK at Shepperton Studios in Surrey, UK, 1976. This page: **AC/DC,** Shepperton Studios shoot while the band were playing for four nights at Marquee Club, Soho, London, 1976.

AC/DC

This was the band's first photo shoot in the UK. I was asked by Warner Brothers Records' PR to do a session of this new group at my studio in Kensington Church Street while they were doing a residency at the Marquee Club in Wardour Street. The shoot didn't go well as they weren't up to participating for more than half an hour before they ripped the background paper to the floor. The contact sheet is the one set up I managed to produce in our brief encounter! The following week I was able to produce some great location images of the band on the back lot of Shepperton film studios.

WHAM!

In spring 1984 I was sent on an assignment by You magazine to Provence, France to photograph Andrew Ridgeley and George Michael of Wham!, who were recording an album in a remote studio. Writer Mick Brown had been briefed by his editor to try and find some scandalous story as the band were riding high in the UK charts. We arrived at the weekend when they were taking a break in recording. Both Mick and myself soon struck a relaxed working relationship with the young stars. The location was idyllic and weather good so every photo session over the stay was productive. Indeed, You used the shots on the cover and a major story in the glossy Sunday supplement. I remember having to support writer Brown's flattering copy, as the editors of the magazine were convinced it had to be a bad boy story.

Shortly after publication I was asked by Simon Napier-Bell, Wham!'s manager, if the band might be able to use the photographs on their next 12" single cover. I agreed and for the next three or so years I became Wham!'s official photographer. In the UK I would shoot stills on the marathon video shoots, which would start at 10am and often go on through the night, finishing with a walking dead crew at 9.59am the next day to avoid paying another day's fees. My photographs were used on record covers, picture discs and general press releases. I guess the highlight of my time with the boys was when I was asked to be their photographer for the 1985 tour of China and Hong Kong. This was a big deal as they were the first western rock band to tour the People's Republic; even the Rolling Stones and Queen had been refused. A large crew of musicians, management, road crew, press core and film crew, led by director Lindsay Anderson, departed London Gatwick airport on a British Caledonian DC10 on route to Hong Kong. The gigs in Hong Kong were uneventful, not unlike a London shows, however things were completely different in Beijing.

WHAM!, George and Andrew on the Great Wall when on the first western band's tour of The People's Republic, 1985.

Left: **WHAM!,** George & Andrew walking in a vineyard south of France taking a break from recording, 1984. This page, top: **ANDREW RIDGELEY OF WHAM!,** with red army soldiers. On Great Wall of China, 1985. This page, bottom: **ANDREW RIDGELEY OF WHAM!,** with flag of China, 1985.

On arrival, officials met us at the airport and I travelled with the band and road manager in an enormous Zil limo, which seemed not to have to stop for red traffic lights as we made our way through the scowling cyclists in the city centre. The temperature was freezing and there were plumes of brown dust. The city looked like one vast building site and there was little evidence of green shoots on the few trees despite it being April. Our new modern hotel could have been in any city; lots of glass, concrete and chrome. Life on tour with any band has a definite routine. It works like this: late lunch, soundcheck, hang around the venue, live concert, back to hotel bar, dinner, hotel club, bed. Now as a photographer, especially on my first trip to China, I used the mornings to take a look around the city. I also had to persuade Andrew and George to go to a few interesting locations for photo sessions, not the easiest to negotiate if they had hit the sack at 4am!

I was helped in my quest for interesting photo calls by the Chinese, who arranged a visit to the Great Wall, and the British press contingent who were given a brief session at the gates of the forbidden city. I was not flavour of the month with the Fleet Street snappers as I had access to all areas on the tour. The gig in Beijing was a strange affair, held in a workers' sports hall with the front rows of seats obviously reserved for party officials, military officers with big hats and their families. Fan reaction to the gig was non existent. I guess nobody wanting to show public enjoyment.

I continued to work with the guys but they split in 1986. I worked on George's 'I Want Your Sex' video and shoot and did a portrait session for Andrew to launch his acting career. It all came to an end when I was asked to return from an assignment in Portugal to photograph the finale party for Wham! I couldn't walk away from the project I was working on and the phone never rang again. It proved to be a turning point in my career. I had never aimed to be a middle-aged rock photographer and my diary was full of assignments from Sunday supplements, automobile magazines and car manufacturers, so with the odd exception in the 1990s, I ended what had been a fantastic fifteen years of Rock fest.

"I TRAVELLED WITH THE BAND AND ROAD MANAGER IN AN ENORMOUS ZIL LIMO, WHICH SEEMED NOT TO HAVE TO STOP FOR RED TRAFFIC LIGHTS."

MARTYN GODDARD

BRYAN FERRY

Working as a contributor for the Telegraph Sunday magazine in the 1970s and 80s, I never knew what assignment would come my way but because of my past form as a music photographer, the picture desk slipped me nice jobs like this Bryan Ferry profile in 1982. The shoot followed a Telegraph formula, which was a photo shoot at the subject's home then accompanying the celebrity on a foreign trip.

The first shoot at Bryan's Chelsea house was a little frosty but at the time I was sharing a studio with a friend whose wife was a mover and shaker and knew Phil Manzanera of Roxy Music. That helped to break the ice and I was able to shoot a nice set of portraits. Then it was off to Rome for the weekend with Roxy Music for a promotional tour.

PETE TOWNSEND

This was a dream assignment, to spend a couple of days with Pete Townsend, a classic fly on the wall reportage with The Who's legendary guitarist, and it proved to be just that. We spent a great couple of days visiting his local haunts in Soho, London; a recording studio, book shop, street market and of course a pub in Wardour St. He was a joy to work with. Once he had agreed to the story, he created an interesting storyboard of his working life and locations for me to record. I just carried one Nikon FM camera and a couple of lenses so shot with minimal fuss, available light and a steady hand despite the pub lunch.

This page: **BRYAN FERRY,** the Roxy Music front man at home in Chelsea, London, 1982. Right: **PETE TOWNSEND,** recording studio in Soho, London, 1980.

U2

In the summer of 1979 I received an assignment from the Telegraph Sunday magazine to photograph a feature by Robin Denslow about the next big thing in rock music. One of the bands was a group from Dublin, U2.

I first met the band at their rented house in Orme Place, Notting Hill, a very desirable address even in the 1970s. Talking over and drinking bad coffee we worked out a plan for the shoot. The location was a bit on the ritzy side so I decided to shoot a sort of story board of what we all imagined a student let to look like, the room untidy with the odd guitar propped up against the furniture and the band members looking like they lived in the place rather than posed in a studio set. We all enjoyed the photo session, which was good, as the next day I travelled to Leeds University to produce photographs at the student union gig.

I arrived at the sound check and it was obvious to me that the stage lighting was not going to hack it for the glossy Sunday supplement, so I hatched a plan where I would produce a couple of on the road type images using my own lighting. The first shot was of U2 in the cab of their VW tour van, the image shot at night with all the accumulated trash from the drive up the M1 from London. The second set-up was on the side of the stage just before the band's performance, which was timely, as all four were fired up and we shot the images in a few minutes. The set of images worked out great and U2 did indeed go on to super stardom. The band remembered the shoot and included the photographs in their book 'U2 by U2'.

U2, rented house in Orme Place
Bayswater, London, 1979.

SPANDAU BALLET

In May 1981, the Sunday Express magazine's art editor Tom Reynolds phoned with an assignment. He asked me to accompany Spandau Ballet on their first promo tour to the USA for five days in New York – and by the way, the writer would be a certain Paula Yates. It took me all of two nano seconds to accept the assignment because I had enjoyed working with North London's New Romantics on several photo shoots for record covers a year or so before. The band was committed to image and style regarding photography and dress. One shoot involved driving five hours to a beach in North Wales, changing in the sand dunes, followed by a couple of hours photography then a five hour return drive. I remember sitting in a motorway café at midnight with members of the band enthusing about what we hopefully had achieved. I was just knackered!

On arrival in the Big Apple we had to hit the ground running as we were taken from the airport to our hotel with the Chrysalis Record's A&R saying, "by the way, we have a dinner booked for 10pm in Soho and then on to an uptown club". The band had been formed from the London club scene so such moonlighting was to be expected. My writer, Ms Yates, was holding court in our booth in the restaurant when the waiter, not accustomed to such a razor edged platinum blond, responded to Paula's jibe "do you like my hairstyle?", with, "ma'am, you should fire your hairstylist!" After dinner we all jumped in a couple of limos to head uptown. I missed most of the proceedings taking a cab back to the restaurant to recover my prized Leica camera, left under my seat in all the fuss of the dining experience!

SPANDAU BALLET,
Brooklyn, New York, 1981.

JETHRO TULL

In 1979 my PR friend at Chrysalis Records suggested that the Telegraph Sunday magazine might like a profile story on progressive rock band Jethro Tull's front man Ian Anderson, who had just become the laird of an enormous Scottish estate, Strathaird on the Isle of Skye. The editor agreed so I flew to the far north and stayed in the Broadford Hotel. The estate was about 15 miles from my hotel along a single-track road, with Loch Siapin to the left and the beautiful Black Cuillin mountains ahead. The estate manager at the building site that was Strathaird House greeted me and we drove in a Land Rover to meet Ian at the new fish farm being constructed in the loch. The manager waxed lyrical about Ian Anderson being a real laird, an owner who was improving the estate with much needed capital to start sustainable hill farming and fishing, unlike the Dutch farmers who at the time had purchased highland estates thinking they could tame the wild landscape to create agribusiness.

The weather closed in and it rained but Ian and I spent a great day photographing all over the estate. There was no shortage of locations; in one rock-pocked and marshy field a herd of highland cattle provided a suitable addition to the photographs. Ian drove me all over the estate in an old 4x4, never once driving on public roads. Important that, as Ian didn't have a driving licence. "Never had time to take my test. I have been touring most of my adult life and have always been driven." Shona, Ian's wife, was the driver of the family.

The shoot was a great success. Jetho Tull toured extensively and had always produced lavish tour programmes, full of original photography and stories. Ian believed that the fans deserved a quality product for the £10 normally charged for such merchandise at gigs, which was quite a price in the late 1970s.

Later, Ian contacted me and asked if I would spend a day at Pinewood studios where the band was in rehearsals to shoot the programme and single covers for the 'Stormwatch Tour'. I agreed and it turned out to be a twenty year collaboration. Ian was great to work with as he was a terrific art director and we created interesting images, set ups and live shots in the sound stage where the band was rehearsing for the tour. It was also a labour of love in a way, as back in my student days I had spent many a night at the legendary progressive rock club Friars in Aylesbury before the Punk and New Wave revolution of 1976.

Left, top: **IAN ANDERSON OF JETHRO TULL,** live gig, 1987.
Left, bottom: **IAN ANDERSON,** photographed on his Strathaird Estate, Isle of Skye, 1979.

ELTON JOHN

The photo shoot with Elton John in Antigua and Montserrat for the 'Empty Garden' single cover and press photography for the 'Jump Up' album January 1982.

In January 1982, I was on a roll with Elton John's Rocket Record Company and was asked to fly to Antigua to photograph him. Accompanied by Laura, the company PR, we eventually ended up at the beach hotel where Elton was sponsoring a local tennis tournament. At a meeting with Elton's road manager the atmosphere was rather negative. Elton had fallen out with the hotel management after being asked to queue for his BBQ on the Tuesday night because the kitchen was closed. Now that might be fine for your average guest but not for the rock icon that was sponsoring the tennis bash! We were tactfully asked to scout out locations for the shoot and check in with Elton's team daily for an update.

The reason for being summonsed to the Caribbean was to shoot a cover for Elton's upcoming single 'Empty Garden (Hey Hey Johnny)' and press photography for the 'Jump It' LP. Laura and I bounced around the sun soaked island in a Mini Moke, checking out locations that we might use but at the daily meetings it was becoming obvious it would be the hotel beach or nothing. On the fifth day the weather was great and all was set for the shoot until Elton decided he had to listen to the commentary of Watford v West Ham in the 4th round of the FA Cup. The road manager, sensing desperation on Laura's part and resignation on mine, said Elton was recording at AIR Studios, Montserrat, on Sunday morning and we were invited to fly over and shoot the cover during the lunch break. The song, Empty Garden, was a tribute to the late John Lennon with whom Elton had sung a duet at Madison Square Garden, New York, in 1974.

Unfortunately on our arrival, Montserrat looked more like Morecambe on a wet winter's morning than a sub tropical island. The studio pool was the location and for about an hour I had Elton John at my beck and call, which became a bit of a work out as the album title involved a fair bit of jumping! One hour's work in a week but a whole lot of planning and anguish. Elton flew off to New York and I to London. The single was released and went to 13 in the US charts. Laura had her press shots and her job!

ELTON JOHN, AIR Studios Montserrat while recording 'Jump', 1982.

PEOPLE

1975 – 2016

DAVID HOCKNEY, the artist
photographed in his studio in
Notting Hill, London, 1977.

This page: **PETER BLAKE,** artist
home studio in London, 1982.
Right: **VIVIENNE WESTWOOD,**
fashion designer with punk
credentials photographed in her
store in London, 1985.

This page: **ANDY WARHOL,** at
a party with Nick Lowe, New York, 1978.
Right: **ANDY WARHOL,** at a party with
Dave Edmonds, New York, 1978.

This page: **TERRY GILLIAN,**
Hampstead Home, London, 1978.
Right: **JAY LENO,** Mr Leno's garage
Burbank, California, USA, 1999.

FAST CARS

1978 – 2000

BUGATTI TYPE 57SC ATLANTIC,
Ralph Lauren collection car
photographed in Essex Massachusetts,
USA, 1991 (Automobile magazine).

EDITORIAL

1976 – 2016

ALFA ROMEO B.A.T.7 1954, Alfa Romeo B.A.T cars on the lawn at Pebble Beach Concours Carmel, California, USA, 1989 (Supercar Classics).

CAR MAGAZINE AND SUPERCAR CLASSICS

Story published in Car photo special, 1985

The Navajo Indian earthquake-watcher, monitoring instruments on the infamous San Andreas Fault in the hills behind San Francisco, politely but very firmly refused to allow Martyn Goddard to take his photograph. Instead, he gave Martyn a cold beer and they chatted for a while, which eased the pain of the refusal. It was the first time in the ebullient photographer's I2 year-old career that a potential subject had positively and definitely refused to be captured on film.

Something of a blow, Martyn recalls with a wry smile, for he was perfect material to supplement a raft of other shots taken on assignment for the Sunday Telegraph magazine.

A setback, that, but not one to daunt Martyn Goddard. In just over a decade his job has taken him all around the world, photographing all kinds of things and people under all kinds of circumstances. He is always on the move, shooting mostly editorial pictures, confidently, smoothly and very reliably. An imaginative physics teacher with a pinhole camera fired Martyn's interest at secondary school and, with advice from a photographer cousin, he planned his career from that point. A three-year course at the Harrow College of Technology and Art enabled him to major in illustrative and fashion photography before working as a freelance assistant to try to grasp the nitty-gritty of the business and establish some worthwhile contacts. That, too, went according to plan and in 1973 Martyn was earning his food shooting junior fashions for Fob 208, then on to assignments with rock stars. So successful were these that their agents booked him for publicity pictures and eventually record covers.

"That was a really exciting time – it was vibrant and I loved every minute of it. In fact, I still shoot record covers for Eddie Grant, which means that there are times of the year when I virtually commute to Barbados, where he lives and works. And I have just done a tour of China with Wham," says Martyn.

Although a dedicated motoring man, Martyn did not have a single car picture in his portfolio when he came through Car's door in 1977 to show art director Wendy Harrop his work. She unhesitatingly assigned him to shoot a Lancia Stratos feature in Wiltshire, which lasted from six in the morning until nine at night in pouring rain and bitter cold. Far from quivering at the memory of it, Martyn remembers it with affection: "We got a nice set of photographs because of the weather, not despite it: there's nothing worse than trying to take pictures on a bright sunny day." The quintessential location photographer. He is uncompromising in his view: "Shooting vehicles in studios is just not on: for me at least. I turn down assignments like that because I don't like them, just as I will refuse jobs when there's insufficient time to do them properly. The criteria is that the pictures the client gets must be of the standard that you put in your own portfolio, regardless of how much you are being paid. Money has nothing to do with it."

"Variety is the freelance's forte and that's what keeps up my enthusiasm level, but I am not interested in sports photography and football is definitely out. I would much rather do an interesting job for a struggling young firm than earn a bundle of money doing something I was not happy with. Sometimes you have to offset the low-paid jobs against the ones that are more lucrative, but it usually works out satisfactorily in the end."

Always outgoing but never extrovert, Martyn is a great believer in personal contact. His good relationships in the music industry, for example, have meant that he can deal directly with clients rather than through agents.

"Getting on with people is so important in this business. If you cannot get on with people then it not only blows your own chance of doing the job well, but also wrecks the efforts of other people," says Martyn. "Quite simply, if there is no chemistry there will be no result. On big, important jobs which can involve teams of people, the photographer needs to be able to generate enthusiasm along the line. Without that, all is lost."

As a person who has photographed a vast communal cross-section, Martyn has very definite ideas about the way it should be done: "No matter who it is, you have to become their instant friend so that you can both relax and get on with taking the pictures. It can be the Duke of Edinburgh, a street-sweeper, a Member of Parliament, David Hockney or the Aga Khan: they are all ordinary people underneath. What makes them seem different is the hype that goes on around them, so that once you're clear of that things start going smoothly."

"I know a lot of photographers don't rate this, but I think that dressing for the occasion is vital. Anyone who goes on a CAR shoot without his wellies and a waterproof jacket stands a great risk of not fitting in with the job in hand. Likewise, wearing a T-shirt and jeans to photograph Royalty at Buckingham Palace makes you a misfit, too, so that those on opposite sides of the camera feel out of place."

A prolific worker, Martyn has equipped himself with the communications paraphernalia of the '80s and always seems to be ready to break into a run to get to the next location on time. He would find it unbearable to be late for an appointment and is a considerable motor vehicle consumer. Brought up on motorcycles, he taught himself to drive in a 1938 Austin saloon that he and his father rebuilt. Martyn even took his driving test in it. After a variety of secondhand cars, he bought a Volkswagen Golf, followed by two Matra-Simca Rancho ("Talbot absolutely wasted those Ranchos – they were so practical and had such potential that they should have evolved to 2.0 litres and 4wd"), and then a succession of Volkswagen Sciroccos, the last two to GTI specification: "I decided that I just couldn't face a Euro box so the Sciroccos proved to be an excellent compromise. I do at least 30,000 miles a year; I need working cars that are fun and genuinely useable as well as reliable. The choice of car is important to photographers – if they get it wrong they will find out quickly enough."

Martyn's motoring activities are not confined to his workhorses, however. Due to an error in some travel arrangement, he once went to Germany 24 hours too early. When European editor Georg Kacher arrived in the evening, they filled in time looking at the small advertisements in a local paper, discovered a Citroën SM at a good price and ended up knocking on a door of a sleepy dealer late at night. Three weeks later, Georg Kacher brought the car to Britain and Martyn has been worshipping at the bumpers of the bronze SM ever since, polishing it, maintaining it, cherishing it and, in the summer months, driving it.

The Citroën SM is one of Martyn's few relaxations, for he is a devoted photographer who always carries at least one camera with him, usually a tiny full-frame 35mm Minox, for taking

"A PROLIFIC WORKER, MARTYN HAS EQUIPPED HIMSELF WITH THE COMMUNICATION PARAPHERNALIA OF THE '80S AND ALWAYS SEEMS TO BE READY TO BREAK INTO A RUN TO GET TO THE NEXT LOCATION."

FORD SHELBY COBRA COUPES 427 1965 & 289 1964, Shelby Daytona Coupes at speed on a test track in Wisconsin, USA, 1990 (Supercar Classics).

PORSCHE 928, farmyard in
Berkshire, my whippet 'Dart'
speeding past the Porsche, 1982
(Car magazine).

Above, from left: **FERRARI 365 1969,**
Steel stockyard in Oakland, California,
USA, 1991 (Supercar Classics, Japan).
CADILLAC CONVERTIBLE 1960,
Outside the Preston Tucker house Ypsilanti,
Michigan, USA, 1990 (Supercar Classics).
CITROEN DS19 1964, Place Vendome,
Paris, France, 1990 (Supercar Classics).
BUGATTI TYPE 1926, Taga Florio pit
complex Sicily, 1982 (Car magazine).

quick candid shots: "Reportage type pictures are fairly easy,"
says Martyn. "You have to be patient and pictures will come to
you – sit on a park bench and people won't even notice that you
are taking pictures of them but if you point a camera at them
at eye level they certainly will." He was once allowed to enter
a monastery to shoot a picture story but only on the condition
that he did not attempt to stop the monks going about their
business. "So I just waited and eventually the pictures I wanted
literally stepped into the viewfinder frame."

The quick candid photograph is not really Martyn Goddard's
style. He enjoys carefully arranging the subject matter and
meticulously preparing the scene for the fraction of a second
it takes to expose the film. Martyn does not see photographs
as the be all and end all: "They become more fascinating when
words are involved on the printed page," he declares. "I try to
visualise how the art director could use the pictures and shoot
accordingly. Words and pictures complement each other: one
element encourages the other to be seen and absorbed. That's

why I'm against books that are purely photographic. The eye is
not sufficiently attracted to the page for it to be totally effective."

Nonetheless, Martyn readily admits to admiration of pictures
atone: "Lartigue's famous photograph of the Edwardian racing
car sums up the car in a single shot. It's a truly remarkable image,
made even more so by the equipment Lartigue was using. Of
course, Lartigue was brilliant for all kinds of real life reportage
pictures - most of them long before the Leica was invented."
Martyn also has great respect for the fashion photographer
Norman Parkinson, enjoying something of a revival at the
moment, as well as the surrealist photographer Edward Weston
who produced some remarkable pictures in the United States
in the 1930s. Martyn also delights in the work of Angus McBean,
whose images in the '30s so annoyed the surrealist painters
that they tried to sue him.

Significantly, Martyn recently acquired a large-format brass
and rosewood Gandolfi field camera with 90mm, 150mm and
210mm lenses about which he claims to be learning more

"MARTYN DOES NOT SEE PHOTOGRAPHS AS THE BE ALL AND END ALL; THEY BECOME MORE FASCINATING WHEN WORDS ARE INVOLVED ON THE PRINTED PAGE."

every time he uses it. At the moment he likes to bring it into action for portrait work where, he says, it tends to bemuse the sitters (mostly company directors) who are more used to staring down the barrel of a much smaller format lens. He also has a Hasselblad outfit: "It's 20 years-old, bought secondhand, and has 50, BO and 150mm lenses plus three film backs and a Polaroid back. A marvellous piece of equipment in its own right."

His other equipment is Nikon: F3s with motor drives and an FM2, backed up with a wide range of lenses including a 16mm fisheye, a 20mm, a 35mm 1.4 (a favourite optic), a 55mm macro, a 70-150 zoom, a 300mm, a 500mm mirror reflex unit and, he says, the most important item of equipment, a sturdy tripod. The camera bodies wear out in around three years, but are generally reliable: "The only time I have been let down was at the Victoria Falls in Zimbabwe when my equipment got absolutely soaked by the mist and spray. So much moisture got into the electronics of the F3 that it died and even after drying in the hot sun it refused to revive."

He uses filters as necessary, mostly the polarising type and neutral graduated filters: "With colour work you have to be able to control the image within the camera and the finished result should never need retouching." For black-and-white photography, Martyn uses Ilford's FP4 and HP5 film, but Fuji 50 and 400 are being used increasingly for colour jobs. Occasionally he will opt for 1000ASA for its coarse grain structure and admits to having a love/hate relationship with Kodachrome which he believes is at its best when used with flash.

A tireless enthusiast for photography, Martyn has involved himself in fewer than six major exhibitions and hopes to do more in the future. Meanwhile, he is returning to fashion work after a long break, but this time to direct a video of Arabella Pollen clothes for showing in a large chain of Japanese shops. He plans to do four videos a year. Although he hopes to become more involved with this type of work in the future, Martyn is unlikely to give up still photography. Rather, he sees the moving image as an extension of, and as a complement to, his existing work.

This page: **GROUP OF LANCIA STRATOS CARS OF 1970S PLUS THE 2010 RECREATION,** location Paul Ricard circuit France, 2010 (Octane magazine). Next page: **CISITALIA 202 1948,** Ex Tazio Nuvolari car photographed in a village near Bologna, Italy, 2008 (Octane magazine).

OCTANE MAGAZINE AND ME

Original copy by Martyn Goddard, 2016

In 2002, I was crawling around on the floor in the paddock at Silverstone photographing a row of gorgeous Bentley Continentals that were at the GP race circuit to celebrate the 50th anniversary of the model. A voice from above asked if he could have a word when I had a minute. It was Robert Coucher, a former editor of Classic Cars magazine. He talked about the glory days of Supercar Classics magazine and how he was hatching an idea for a similar magazine focusing on the upper end of the classic car market but with a few lifestyle and new car twists. Was I interested if this ever came to pass? Yes, was my immediate reply and I continued to photograph Bentleys and forgot all about the encounter.

Octane magazine was founded and the first issue published in May 2003, I may say without any of my images. My first contribution was not an eight page story on some über rare Ferrari or Porsche but a 'day in the life' feature hidden on page 162 of issue 6 on Mike Cross, Jaguar test driver. Things have looked up since those early days for the magazine and myself. Octane has established itself as a benchmark publication covering the top end of the classic car movement with a circulation of 40,000 plus. In fact, whenever I am working on assignment in the USA or Europe, collectors, car owners, restorers, auctioneers and players in the classic car world say they subscribe.

From the back page in 2003, my contributions to Octane have evolved. Connections in America gave me access to some important automobiles such as the Ralph Lauren collection, and the magazine was open to me creating stories, initially collaborating with Phil Llewellin then latterly Dale Drinnon.

In 2004 David Lillywhite gave me the chance to write a road trip story. I had come up with the idea of following the Tour de France cycle race as a fan by motorcycle, so taking a writer was out of the question. This gave me many challenges, not the least being that I am dyslexic. I had never undertaken such a long trip on such a vast motorcycle, the BMW GS1150, and I couldn't speak French. Despite all probability of disaster, I enjoyed my adventure camping up on the cols with bike fans including Begiums, Basques and people from all over the world. The images I was able to capture with copious note taking learned from thousands of miles in the seat next to Phil Llewellin were published in the November 2004 issue entitled 'Chasing the Tour'. That start has led to a catalogue of road trips now undertaken in classic cars that are incredibly rewarding, a chance to travel in the cars I love and work with.

My work with Octane continues with car shoots, 'Gearbox' features and road trips. It's not all plain sailing as the editorial team is small and very busy so communicating is more difficult than talking to my bank via an Indian call centre. On the plus side they are tolerant of the odd Goddard executive decision making. I will often turn up at an event and end up shooting a set of photographs and write up the proceedings. Long may the magazine prosper. 'Fuelling the passion' as it says on the magazine cover.

FIAT TOPOLINO JOLLY 1952,
Coffee stop while driving around
Lake Como Italy, June 2015.

This page: **ALFA ROMEO DISCO SPYDER
VOLANTE BY TOURING OF MILAN 2016,**
supercar on a ferry crossing Lake Como
approaching Bellagio, February 2016.
Right: **MASERATI 250S 1957,** winter photo
shoot near Bologna, 2010 (Octane magazine).

FERRARI MONDIAL COUPE AND SPIDER 1950S, Classic car restoration shop near Bologna, 2010 (Octane magazine).

This page, top: **FERRARI 288 GTOS,**
31 Ferrari GTOs parked at the factory
in Marenello Italy, 1984 (Car & Driver).
This page, bottom: **ENZO FERRARI,**
Press conference at Fiorano Ferrari
test track, 1984 (Car & Driver). Right:
FERRARI F40, F40 photographed at
Fiorano test track, 1987 (Car & Driver).

AMERICAN MAGAZINES

Story published in Automobile magazine, February 2016

Thousands of images taken on hundreds of assignments, choosing my favourite image when asked was daunting. I have contributed to Automobile magazine before it was a magazine, when founding editor David E Davis Jr. asked me to shoot a British sports car in the land of his ancestors, Wales. Why a Panther Kallista was chosen I can't remember but the resulting mock up feature was used in the media pack sent to prospective advertisers.

My chosen photograph of the red 1955 Maserati 300S parked in a piazza in Brescia, Italy before the 2001 Mille Miglia Classic and being admired by a young Italian woman standing with her bicycle, for me ticks all the boxes. It represents my work for Automobile magazine and the ethos of the publication. I try to have a creative input when photographing the cars. It might be action, a dramatic location or as in this image, a person's interaction with the vehicle. Just to photograph the automobile is to record the work of the designer and craftsmen that made it. The shot represents all that is good about Automobile magazine, stories of great or significant cars participating in events or driven on road trips all over the USA, or Europe in this case.

The brief for the Maserati 300S assignment from editor Mark Gillies was typically simple: "I am driving in a Maserati 300S on the Mille Miglia, can you follow and shoot the story."

PORSCHE 959, driving at
speed in Germany. Test top speed
188mph, 1983 (Car & Driver).

"THE MILLE MIGLIA STARTED THAT EVENING IN TORRENTIAL RAIN. WE PHOTOGRAPHERS TOOK REFUGE IN LOCAL CAFÉS USING OUR NAPKINS TO DRY SOAKED NIKON AND CANON CAMERAS."

MARTYN GODDARD

We decided it might be interesting to not only cover the 1000-mile dash around Italy but also incorporate a sort of period road test element to the feature, driving impressions and car details. The plan was that I would chase the Maserati in an Alfa 156 aided by a driver. The image taken in the piazza was shot after scrutineering, in the centre of Brescia where the Mille Miglia started. We were all resting, having an espresso in a bar recovering from Italian tech inspectors, myself trying to shoot details of the engine and interior of the 300S and hundreds of tifosi who just had to look under the hood at the gorgeous straight six Maserati motor. The light was fading into that warm glow that photographers revel in when the signorina, who was cycling across the piazza, stopped to admire the Maserati just parked like any Fiat 500 in any Italian City. At this point I would love to comment that I picked up my camera and in good street photographer fashion captured the shot. Alas, this is not true. I dispatched my young driver to engage the woman in conversation to ask if she would let me take a couple of shots of her with our car. She agreed and afterwards cycled off probably thinking she imagined the whole thing.

The Mille Miglia started that evening in torrential rain. We photographers took refuge in local cafes using their napkins to dry soaked Nikon and Canon cameras. The 300S departed, open to the elements, for what turned out to be a terrific three days of photography. David my driver drove and I navigated a rally within a rally, plotting routes that would place me in the best location to illustrate a great car on a wonderful event. The results were published in the December 2001 issue of Automobile magazine but my favourite image wasn't included in the layout, instead a vertical shot of the car alone in the piazza was the opener.

MASERATI 300S 1955,
photographed in a piazza in Brescia,
Italy, before 2001 Mille Miglia
(Automobile magazine).

LANCIA DELTA INTEGRALE EVO II 1995, Monte Carlo Rally stage in the French Alps, 2016 (Automobile magazine).

ROAD TRIPS

1986 – 2013

KEY TO THE HIGHWAY

Published January 2015, Octane magazine

An indelicate whiff of oil-ooze onto exhaust manifold must have been reaching the valet parking desk of the distinguished New Orleans hotel even as I killed the ignition. But at least the water pump hadn't puked, yet, and the attendant remained oh-so professionally composed as we skirted Caddie's well-seasoned flanks to collect my luggage. Then he noticed the license plate, and with the faintest undertone of wonderment, he asked "You drove this car down here from Tennessee?"

"Yeah, man," I say, "and I'm going up Highway 61 through Mississippi like the old Blues Men did, one club at a time, and on to Chicago, and I'm gonna write a story about it." I give the trunk lid a little pat and reach out the keys. "Put my baby someplace nice, will you?"

There is the slightest undecided pause, and he smiles, a wondrous, reassuring smile of the impromptu co-conspirator. "Don't worry, sir," he says, "I'll do your baby right," nodding toward a front-row spot between a Lexus and a Merc, "and if we can help any way whatsoever, you ask for me personally." And he shakes my hand.

It is, I believe, a very Southern thing to do. Native Southerners, whether they're Black like my new friend or Poor White Trash like me, understand intimately about leaving home and family in search of a better life, or in many Black circumstances, any life at all, and we have a gut-deep appreciation for the quintessential people's liberation weapon that often made it possible, the cheap used car.

Factor in whatever Southern mystery DNA that originated most of world's popular music genres, and following the trail to the Chicago recording studios where the Mississippi Delta Blues giants inspired musical generations yet unborn becomes a sacred trust. Frankly, I wasn't sure any non-Southerner could ever fully get that, even well-travelled British photographer and Blues fanatic Martyn Goddard – any more than I as a transplanted American will ever understand their whole God

Save the Queen obsession. So from the day we hatched our Blues trip idea, I knew the only car that could bring everything together.

It would have to be a Cadillac, and the cheapest possible cheap Cadillac with a few miles remaining. A "fake it 'til you make it" car that might bestow some small Blues Man credit (I drive a Cadillac, baby…), if viewed from a dark, squinty distance. About a grand should do it, I thought, and asked my friend and former racing partner Stan Heath back in Knoxville to keep an eye open. Two weeks later he sent an email. "Found a car," it read, "1981 Coupe de Ville, $1,000 all-in, photos attached." I studied them for a full minute, and replied "buy it".

Highly skilled repair work was naturally required when I flew in to collect our prize. I hammered the motor and tracks on the jammed power driver's seat until they surrendered in terror, and sweet-talked my ex-boss Lowell Arp, service manager at Twin City Buick, out of some second-hand tires. After much soul searching, I also splurged on a 20-buck boom box to offset the radio-shaped hole in the dash, and set forth to meet Martyn at the jumping off point in New Orleans.

Despite the city's jazz association, we picked New Orleans for more than just a convenient airport; it was a trendsetter in establishing music as a viable profession for Blacks in the traditional Deep South. In the immediate post – Civil War period, two critical civic assets made it a natural magnet town: a booming, legal French Quarter red light district called Storyville needing musical entertainment, and easy access to a poor ex-slave culture that had stayed sane over three centuries mostly through music.

It was a symbiotic system that worked well for years, until WW1 when the Army squashed Storyville to save doughboys at the local base from immorality until they could be shot in France. C'est la guerre, I guess, literally.

The magnet tradition continues, though, and Martyn and I spend a memorable afternoon in the day lounge of a huge name-brand McClub listening to a talented lad from Seattle named Colin Lake, lately come down to learn the Blues trade. Early in the following am, we hit old U.S. 61, the renowned pre-Interstate artery from New Orleans clear to Bob Dylan's childhood Minnesota doorstep, heading to the true heart of the Blues, the Mississippi Delta.

The first hundred miles nearly turned us turn back around. Highway 61 tours some less scenic sections of Baton Rouge, not improved by the type of Gulf Coast frog-strangler that often results in CNN tornado footage. Then, just north of BR, on a long, bleak dead-end road comes the biggest downer of anyone's Blues Adventure: the Louisiana State Penitentiary at Angola.

Top: **CADILLAC COUPE DE VILLE 1981,** Dale removing punctured tyre at B&B in Indianola, 2014 (Octane magazine). Bottom: **CADILLAC COUPE DE VILLE 1981,** interior on the road, 2014 (Octane magazine).

Huddie Ledbetter, a.k.a. Lead Belly, an acknowledged Founding Father, did time there, and it's worth noting that when '30s Library of Congress musicologists John and Alan Lomax wanted the oldest, purest forms of African-American music, they went to Angola – discovering Lead Belly – and they weren't the last. Equally noteworthy is that while America's black population is roughly 14-percent, its black prison population is 40-percent. Angola is as grim as grim gets, and for once we don't linger for the perfect photo; we don't even stop rolling. Martyn grabs a pic through the windshield and I romp the throttle.

Several miles thereafter pass silently. We have different Blues appreciations, as you'd expect from different backgrounds; Martyn is a former pro rock 'n roll snapper, a life-long student of the Blues, listens to them every day, and his proudest family possessions are a John Lee Hooker autograph and a '60s photo of his sister with Little Walter. Meanwhile, I don't know jack, but I grew up amid the poverty, racism and inequality that produced the Blues in the first place, and my love of them just feels somehow innate. For both of us, however, a slap from the ugly side of Blues reality is a thoroughly sobering experience.

Fortunately, the car soldiers along as if in compensation. The '81 Cadillac V8-6-4 was a techno disaster, rarely combining correct cylinder selection with correct opportunity, but it's worlds better once stuck in permanent V8 mode, and a smooth, steady 55-60 works fine, interrupted only by interminable fluid refills, the master cylinder being worryingly one of them. Nonetheless, the mileage computer, still spot-on after 32 years, shows a

respectable 18 mpg average when the long day's drive lands us in the Delta town of Indianola.

Officially, no one knows where or when the Blues began; unofficially, this area around Indianola, Clarksdale, Greenwood, this might as well be it, based on its sheer impact since Blues music reached national white recognition in the 1920s. B.B. King is from Indianola, Muddy Waters grew up on nearby Stovall Plantation and Alan Lomax famously recorded him there in 1941; Bessie Smith died tragically in Clarksdale and Robert Johnson sold his soul to the Devil at the Clarksdale crossroads of Highways 61 and 49. As this is among the poorest areas in the poorest state in the USA, some of that Blues provenance could also prove useful going forward.

The smart money here is now on Blues tourism, and with reason. At Poor Monkey, one of the few old-time country juke joints left and virtually unfindable by any but locals, there are super-cool European 20-somethings with tight black tee-shirts and stylish shoes, never mind there's no live music anymore.

Likewise at heart-poundingly authentic Red's Lounge in Clarksdale, where the Saturday night attractions are 14-year-old guitar genius Christone "Kingfish" Ingram, and significantly older vocalist Josh "Razorblade" Stewart ("Razorblade, 'cause he always look sharp"), the crowd is almost entirely tourists, both foreign and domestic. With memories of a considerably different Mississippi, I don't care, either, whether that's the result or the cause of Indianola's new B.B. King Museum or the

Left: **BLUES CLUB IN NEW ORLEANS,** 2014 (Octane magazine). This page: **CADILLAC COUPE DEVILLE 1981,** Outside Sun Studios Memphis, Tennessee, USA, 2014 (Octane magazine).

FRONT MAN 'RAZOR BLADE',
playing at 'Reds' Blues Club
Clarksdale. Mississippi, 2014
(Octane magazine).

Left, top: **DALE,** reading local paper
in Natchez, Mississippi. Left, bottom:
CADILLAC, parked in fronted BB King
street art in Indianola, Mississippi. This
page: **BEAL STREET,** Memphis, Tennessee.

steadily revitalizing, Blues-themed Clarksdale downtown.
To me, it's a sign God does love Mississippi, and all is forgiven.

But Blues tourism is nothing new up Route 61 in Memphis.
Beale Street was an early Tennessee equivalent to Storyville,
except the prostitution wasn't legal, and I can remember
awesome Blues nights on Beale even in the Bad Old Southern
Days. It must be the planet's only Blues-oriented big city
festival district, and not that far off Beale is Sun Studios, where
Mississippi native and Blues fan Elvis Presley perfected the art of
Black Blues attitude inside White Top-40 skin.

The studio that matters personally, though, is 150 miles away
in Muscle Shoals, Alabama: Fame Studios, where Duane Allman
made his breakthrough in 1968, legend says, by living in a tent
outside until they'd let him play. Since Duane and brother
Greg were white boys born in Tennessee, had long hair
and hippie clothes, the critics called the Allman Brothers' music
"Southern Rock".

At the core, though, it was Blues, and the perfect Blues for white
kids and black kids who were best friends in the late '60s South
to share in the only place we felt safe – in the car, usually
a cheap used one, always moving. Duane's Statesboro Blues
sounds as good in the Fame parking lot, too, as it did when Vic
and I were 18.

After Memphis, there's a long road indeed to Chicago, and on
boring, featureless Interstate. The Caddie is still going strong,
so strong we're talking silly about keeping it, but not so strong
that I dare push over 60, and the anticipation of Getting There
has a certain poignancy. Chicago was the ultimate magnet town,
really, for the entire multi-million Great Migration of hopeful
African-American Southerners to the North, and tonight we'll
see the part the Blues migrants most hoped for. Buddy Guy
left Louisiana for Chicago in 1957 at age 21, got his first record
contract a year later, and became a superstar.

Eric Clapton has called him "the best guitar player alive", and
his club, Buddy Guy's Legends, is world famous, and completely
packed on a slow Tuesday night. Career fulfilment doesn't get
any better in the Blues business, brother.

With mere hours left before Martyn flies home, a visit to Willie Dixon's Blues Heaven Foundation, formerly Chess Records and a lynchpin of that same Blues business seems a nice wrap-up. It's where the Delta immigrants recorded new electrified Chicago Blues that wowed The Stones and Clapton and Jimmy Page, and a mention to our guide, Willie's grandson Keith, of seeing Kingfish in Clarksdale gets such a nod of the Blues cred I've been coveting I hardly notice his subsequent comments on Little Walter climbing those very stairs over there. But Martyn notices.

I've never, ever seen him ignore his camera before, but he does now, and for a long time I just listen to them chatter about Little Walter's '64 European tour, Muddy Waters playing Manchester, and John Lee Hooker on the BBC. Until it clicks. Of course he Gets It, you moron. The Blues to him was a sudden blast of fresh air into a stale world, and of possibilities never before imagined, and they changed his life forever. For some, exactly like the Beatles coming to America; for others, like going North to Chicago. Or chasing hope with a cheap used car.

Left: **CADILLAC COUPE DE VILLE 1981,** Po Monkey's Juke joint Merigold, Mississippi.
This page: **CADILLAC COUPE DE VILLE 1981,** French Quarter New Orleans, Louisiana, USA.

MONTEREY OR BUST

Published December 1986, Automobile magazine

The Mercedes-Benz Racing Cars, Essex, Massachusetts – Alex Finigan doesn't own a Mercedes-Benz 300SL. Few people do: only 1400 of the spectacular Gullwings were built from 1954 to 1957. But Finigan has been restoring them for a decade, most recently for Paul Russell at the Gullwing Service Company, thirty-five miles north of Boston in Essex.

There are two parts to Alex Finigan: He is the worst sort of car freak, one who has a photographic memory and who has twenty car magazines delivered to his house every month. And Finigan is a full-blown nut case. Sha Na Na on speed. "We never see Alex down," say his co-workers. "In the shop, he's a howl. If he hears a song he likes on the radio, he puts it up real loud and sings at the top of his lungs. Alex really enjoys life. "I'm a fourteen-year-old," says Finigan, eyes crossed and tongue out, "with forty years' experience."

You need to know a little of Paul Russell's philosophy on the art of Gullwing restoration to understand why customer Nick Jones loaned Alex Finigan his rare $150,000, aluminum-bodied 1955 Gullwing (number twenty-eight of twenty-nine aluminum Gullwings made) to drive to Monterey. The Gullwing Service Company is not a museum. When the guys come to work and look around the shop (today the work bays hold a 1957 Gullwing, a 1957 Roadster, a 1953 170S, a 1961 Roadster, an aluminum Gullwing belonging to Ralph Lauren, a white 1956 Gullwing, and a chassis believed to be the first Gullwing), they see cars. And their job is to put those cars back on the road in perfect running order – in most cases, better than new. On the subject of concours-quality cosmetics, Paul Russell says: "It seems

nasty to have a guy with white gloves on stick his finger up your tailpipe." Not that the Gullwing Service Company won't or can't do a contours-winning restoration. But to the guys in Essex, the matter of restoring the greatest of Mercedes-Benz production cars goes much deeper than the number of lacquer coats on the car's sensuous skin.

In its day, the 300SL was revolutionary. "With its unsurpassed speed, its acceleration still strong up in the three-figure region, and its exotic good looks and technical features, the 300SL hit the motoring world with the impact of a sledgehammer," wrote Karl Ludvigsen. Mercedes-Benz had never intended to build a production Gullwing. But Max Hoffman, the man responsible for bringing the greatest European marques to America in the Fifties, was enthralled by the 300SL that won the 1952 Carrera Panamericana. He convinced Mercedes-Benz to put the car on the street by promising cash for the delivery of 1000 production 300SLs.

The car debuted before the public at the 1954 New York International Motor Sports Show, showcasing the industry's first production fuel injection system. The 240-horsepower in-line six-cylinder engine used an overhead cam, and the injection pump housed a built-in altimeter and thermostat to compensate for air-density changes. An aluminum intake manifold sprouted ram pipes to each of the cylinders, the brake drums were steel-lined aluminum, vacuum-boosted, and finned for cooling, and the chassis was a tube frame. Mercedes-Benz also advertised optional rear axle ratios that would deliver up to 162 miles an hour at the top end. And it was beautiful.

ROAD TRIP MERCEDES-BENZ
300SLS, driving next to the Great Salt
Lake, Utah, USA, 1986 (Automobile).

**1955 MERCEDES BENZ
300SL,** Chicago Truck stop,
1986 (Automobile).

"For some people, these cars work as art objects," explains Finigan. "For us, they're almost like industrial machine objects. We build our cars to be driven. We pull apart every last nut and bolt; the cars are almost remanufactured. Most of our customers want cars that work, that they can drive 120 miles an hour all day long. If our cars can't do that, they're failures. We don't build cars, put them on stretchers, and haul them to shows.

"The Gullwing Service Company is the kind of place where real people rebuild honest cars for genuine car enthusiasts. Paul Russell's customers believe in his work, pay him by the hour, even. There's a two-year waiting list. And the Gullwing Service Company has the kind of customers who would say, "Sure, drive the car to Monterey for the races." It had in fact, two such customers: Nick Jones and Manfredo Lippmann. So, in honor of the Mercedes-Benz 100th Anniversary celebration at Pebble Beach and Laguna Seca, Alex Finigan, accompanied by his good Pal me, co-workers Jack Daly, Peter Bulkeley, and Bruce Marston, and our fearless f-stop Martyn Goddard, lined up the aluminum Gullwing and a red 1958 Roadster for a week's worth of 500-mile days.

By the morning of our departure, our two-car caravan had grown to include: a white 1957 Roadster that we would drive as far as Chicago; attorney John Perenyi and his black pearl 1955 Gullwing; and the company van, which was hauling a covered trailer full of spare parts sandwiched around a 1960 Roadster that would be delivered to its owner in California. And Finigan had published our route in the 300SL newsletter as a challenge to any other sporting types to put their cars on the road to Monterey.

We had one rule that we promised to abide by: we wouldn't drive the aluminum Gullwing over ninety miles an hour if its side glass was removed, to avoid the possibility of blowing out the Plexiglas rear window. There wasn't too much else to worry about. Let's face it – when you can start with bushel baskets full of parts and finish with a pristine $150,000 Gullwing, you're not going to be racked with worry about the car breaking down.

As with all road trips, this one started out tentatively, the drivers a little on edge as they tuned themselves into the rhythms of their cars and the road. We eased onto the Massachusetts Turnpike, raced to 100mph, slowed to sixty, ran nose to tail, then side by side, until the only real matched set among us, Perenyi and his very own Gullwing, put his foot down and left.

We found him an hour later in a service area with the missing link of a perfect cross-country motorcade – master body man Al Poskus and his sidekick/protégé Johnny Yanakakis. Big, grizzly Al and short, well-muscled Johnny. Thirty-six and twenty-one. Lithuanian and Greek. The body men, in their

lustrous, cream-colored 1969 280SE coupe, were waiting to show us the way. This, of course, could never have been accomplished with a stock 280SE, so Big Al mated a high-performance 250SE head to the 280 block, added a 280SL cam, injectors, and injection pump, and traded a four-speed manual for the automatic to squeeze more revs from the motor.

"Everybody said it wouldn't run," Big Al told us, smiling. "I'm really happy with the way it runs. What are we sitting here for?" And, grinning a demonic grin, he nailed the gas. We finally had our rhythm – to drive fast enough to keep Al in sight.

We could never hope to catch the crazy sucker – the aluminum Gullwing had a 4.11 rear end, good for only about 120 – although we had great fun trying. All four forward gears were jampacked with revs waiting to be tapped. The car was more animal than bird; little of the fury under its hood was muffled from the cockpit, and we fairly had to shout to be heard. At sixty miles per hour the straight six was turning at 3000rpm at eighty 4000, at 100 a lusty bellowing 5000 rpm. We were hooked on the noise at five grand, lungs thrumming in our chest from engine power coursing through the car, but prudence reined us in at around 4000.

Mercedes-Benz had the feel and placement of the pedals and the stout little stick shifter right thirty years ago. And the gauges were clustered tightly within the circle of the large steering wheel. That thin, hard, oversized wheel (a mere 2.0 turns lock to lock) had complete command over our course; it was a little vague through center, but there was no slop in the system. The brute force required to handle the Gullwing's wheel wouldscare off the faint of heart. Conversely, there is a raw physical thrill that comes with expending a large amount of energy to drive a Gullwing with élan. There aren't many thirty-year-old cars you could push like this. The boys had done their job well. They, of course, knew all along what the car would do. I was the one who was completely delirious thinking of the thrill of the week ahead.

"Jack and Bruce and Bunchy (Peter Bulkeley] were the only guys in the shop who wanted to go on this trip," admitted Finigan. "You work on them every day for ten years, you get blasé. It sometimes takes someone else's enthusiasm to spark you." Of which there was plenty. Throughout the miles of road construction on Interstate 80 through New York and Pennsylvania, our rolling auto show made huge points with the construction crews. They always let us through on the tail end of the green flag, thumbs up. At our first fill-up, 412 miles from Essex, the station manager exploded from his office. "Wow! I ain't seen so much money in my life at once. Where'd ya get all them good-lookin' automobiles? I'm gonna take yer picture, girl. Ya prob'ly won't be back here, will ya?"

Left, top: **1955 MERCEDES GULLWING 300SL,** road trip team at Bonneville Utah, USA. Left, bottom: **MERCEDES-BENZ 300SL,** lunch stop in Nevada, USA, 1986 (Automobile magazine). This page: **MERCEDES-BENZ 300SL ROADSTER,** Gullwing mechanic 'Bunchy' photographing 300SL roadster at Bonneville Utah, USA, 1986 (Automobile magazine).

And a state trooper (Ohio, of course) followed us into a truck stop near Cleveland. He was a big one. "Howdy, fellas," he said, pulling on his Big Hat against the broiling sun. The asphalt was literally oozing tar around his feet. "I've got a buddy with a '36 Ford pickup, and he's going to them gullwing doors." After thirty minutes swapping hot rod stories, he promised to keep an eye on the cars while we stopped for lunch. In Ohio, I'm telling you. These cars were definitely magic.

The boys didn't really get heated up until we got to Chicago and found a red Roadster with Ontario plates waiting in our hotel parking lot. By morning, two more Gullwings had materialized. So had our "support" vehicle, which was lagging so far behind that it might as well have been parked back in Essex.

A crowd gathered in the local Denny's parking lot to gawk at the flock of metal birds, while we powwowed over pancakes. The late arrivals had decided not to stop that night with us, but to press on for Bonneville. Finigan and Jack Daly locked eyes.

"Bonneville!" they shouted in unison. "Oh, shit! SPEED WEEK!" It was the first time that the van and trailer, Jack Daly at the wheel, would beat us anywhere. The massive 280SE pulled the rumbling group back onto 1-80. With Big Al leading the way, three-pointed star flattened against the 280's hood, four Gullwings and two red Roadsters flailed the deserted highway, holding first at ninety-five, then 100 miles an hour.

America's early morning vacation traffic might not have known the exact identity of the megabuck machinery barreling past, but it knew that this was something special. Try passing a Good Sam Winnebago at ninety in a Countach and see what digit gets flung up in salute. But it was all thumbs for the 300SLs. While Dad snoozed, Mom honked, and the kids waved furiously.

We found a farmer looking at the cars when we came back from lunch, in Altoona, Iowa. "You boys watch out for cops over to Omaha," he drawled. "They picked me up two months ago. They had an airplane!" he said in disgust. "My Whistler didn't do me a bit of good. I shoulda had it through the roof

"What year is that Mar-cedes?" he asked, squinting at the Gullwing. "I didn't know they used them doors like Da Larryan."

Evening prayers before supper were the same every night:

"Didja see that Bronco on tank treads? Jee-zus!"

"Yeah! And didja see the '65 Bug with chrome zoomies? Jee-zus!" "How 'bout the '36 Ford three-window coupe? Jee-zus!"

The Lancia Zagato. Jee-zus.

The '54 Chevy Bel Air two-door hardtop. Jee-zus.

The '56 Nomad wagon. Jee-zus. The '58 Chevy 4x4 dump truck on eight tractor tires. Jee-zus.

From left: **MERCEDES-BENZ 300SL ROADSTER,**
Alex Finigan driving on freeway in Nevada, USA.
MERCEDES-BENZ 300SL ROADSTER, Alex Finigan
and Jean Lindamood on the freeway heading West, 1986
(Automobile magazine). **MERCEDES-BENZ 300SL,**
Running repairs to Gullwing on freeway in Utah, USA.
MERCEDES-BENZ 300SL'S, Truck stop in Chicago
Illinois, USA, 1986 (Automobile magazine).

"Yeah! Yeah!" hollered Finigan. "Holy shit!"

And the closer we got to Bonneville, the thicker grew the traffic of magnificent machinery. We found Jack Daly and Bruce Marston standing next to the tnick by the entrance to the salt. They were in Bonneville T-shirts and Bonneville baseball caps, and they had installed a Bonneville sticker and a Bonneville license plate bracket on the van. Jack, looking for all the world like a member of ZZ Top, had chunks of salt dribbling from his long red beard. "I kissed the salt," he said sheepishly. Because none of us had been there before, we were stunned to discover that the paved road stopped five miles short of the action. "We can't drive the cars on the salt!" we yelled at each other, as we teetered on the edge of the pavement, dying to get to that point in the distance where a blinding light was moving rapidly across the horizon. Eventually, we bought T-shirts and left, devastated. "We should have hitched.." I began.

"Don't even say it!" Finigan warned.

It was hot now, well over 100 degrees. We had the Gullwing's side windows removed, but the sweat was soaking the towels covering the seats. "I feel like someone sprayed me with Pam," whined Finigan, as I scribbled in my trusty notebook. "Are you writing that you're sweating like a hog?" he asked.

"sweating like a hog…," I scribbled.

It could have been worse. Gullwings were notorious for being as hot as ovens, and the Gullwing Service Company had sprayed

closed-cell foam behind the dashboard and in the channels behind the doors to better insulate the cockpit. They also louvered the rocker bottoms to suck hot air out the bottom of the rocker panels. So we got roasted instead of toasted.

We traded often between the Gullwing and the Roadster, just to experience a little breeze. For the passenger, though, the Roadster was even worse. Its exhaust ran down the right side of the car, and the floor would become hot enough to cook Thanksgiving dinner on. I would swing around in the seat and ride with head on dash and legs up over the trunk, which drove the truckers crazy, according to Big Al's squawking CB.

At first, we thought the heat had caused the Gullwing's only mechanical breakdown: a failure in the auxiliary fuel pump, which we ran to counteract vapor lock during hard driving. The problem proved to be electrical. The truck, of course, was about five hours behind us.

"Twenty grand worth of tools in the truck," groaned Finigan, "and we don't even have a dime to use for a screwdriver."

Martyn Goddard peered around his Nikon, stopped shooting for a moment, and fished around in his camera bag, coming up with his bazillion-blade, full-boat, dee-luxe version of the trusty Swiss Army knife. The boys jumped into action, jury-rigging a hot lead from the pump to a taillight.

"Martyn, do you suppose you'd have a soldering iron in that bag?" asked Jack Daly.

The Roadster experienced a number of niggling problems—a wacky speedo cable, a horn that began honking by itself in Nevada—but nothing that shut the car down. Living with Gullwing and Roadster for a week sparked great debate over which one we'd buy when we won the lottery. The Roadster was certainly an easier car to live with. Its handling was less diabolical than the Gullwing's, thanks to the redesigned low-pivot swing axle assembly and the addition of a horizontally located third coil spring. (This "compensating" coil allowed softer main springs for reduced camber change with no loss of load capacity.) And the Roadster's 3.25:1 rear axle ratio made it a much easier car in which to carry on a conversation. Although muted, the engine still sang. Coming slowly down through the Sierra Nevada from South Lake Tahoe to Sacramento, Jack Daly played between second and third gears to hear the engine's delicious shriek on the rock faces that lined Highway 50. "You could almost feel it smiling," he said later on.

To Bunchy, though, the Gullwing lit the flame. "It makes me feel like I did when I first had my driver's license and didn't want to ever get out of the car."

Crossing the California state line had been bittersweet. The adventure would be history in 300 miles. And, sadly, so would the camaraderie. "I feel like this will be the highlight of my life," said Bunchy, forlornly. "And it's almost over."

We were greeted in Monterey by the not-even-slightly-anxious

Messrs. Jones and Lippmann, and the rest of the Gullwing Service Company, who had come to watch the boss race Nick Jones's Gullwing. (Was there no end to the generosity of Mr. Jones?) There was a moment of uncomfortable tension, as the guys from the shop who had flown to Laguna looked at our tan, laughing group, arms thrown casually around each other, eyes bright. The unasked question was clear on each face: Why didn't I go?

I walked away from my pals at Laguna Seca. Paul Russell would drive our faithful Gullwing to eighth overall in the 300SL race. Bunchy, John Perenyi, Jack Daly, Big Al, and Johnny Yanakakis would drive back. Finigan would fly.

And I would fly to England two days later, sit in a pub wrapped in sweaters drinking an ale with the Le Mans winner Derek Bell, suntan shredding off my face, and hear the echo of Finigan leading the guys through the paddock at Laguna. They were praying again:

"Didja see that '53 Siata 208? Jee-zus!"

"Yeah! And didja see the Type 35 Bugatti? Jee-zus!"

"How 'bout the Birdcage Maserati? Jee-zus!"

"The '64 Alfa GTZ. Jee-zus."

"The '65 Cobra 427. Jee-zus."

"The '59 Stanguellini Formula Junior. Jee-zus."

FORD LOTUS CORTINA MK1
1965, driving away from Bamburgh
Castle Northumberland, 2013
(Octane magazine).

TO THE WILDS OF THE NORTH

Published February 2013, Octane magazine

The pages covering Northumberland in my battered 1996 Philips road atlas were pristine and lacking the scribbled notes the rest of the maps had, denoting good photo locations. The reason, after thirty years of automotive photography, is that this furthest northern region of England has been off my creative radar, a black hole just waiting for discovery on a UK road trip. I had a plan to celebrate the fiftieth anniversary of the Cortina and Ford's heritage collection provided a 1965 Mark 1 Lotus for our adventure, a car that turned a good saloon into a true sports sedan and race car piloted by the likes of Sir John Whitmore and Jim Clarke. I had the good fortune to watch them as a teenager at Silverstone or viewed from my uncle's office window above the Crystal Palace circuit.

Heading up Kentish Town road after departing early from Maison Goddard in Camden Town, the A1 road sign just says, 'The North', our chosen route via this truly British trunk road which does not deviate for the thick end of 300 miles to the Marches of Northumberland. It's a fitting drive for the sports saloon, designed in an era when there were fewer than 100 miles of motorway in the entire UK! A graffiti covered wall in a field off the road signalled, 'You are now leaving the future'. The met office were spot on, torrential rain and road spray battered the little Ford, but to the car's credit the single speed wipers coped with the conditions and the revolutionary 1960s through flow ventilation system produced acceptable front and rear visibility. I commented to Beverley that there was a lot of standing water on the road only to round a curve and see a Mazda MX5 buried in the southbound Armco barrier, causing a ten-mile traffic jam! The Lotus-Cortina has a 14-inch wood rimmed steering wheel and a full set of Smiths round gauges, only lacking a clock. The miles passed before I noticed that the fuel gauge had taken a nosedive – requiring a fuel stop. I filled up with four gallons plus octane booster, so guessed

there was a gauge error because the specification sheets give the car a 10-gallon tank. Lunch continued the retro theme at the OK Diner where we tucked into roadhouse food, no healthy options. We continued north through wind and rain arriving at the Close House hotel and golf club at dusk, the Cortina's vinyl sports seats providing admirable comfort on the journey. We unloaded our luggage from the cavernous boot, parked over a giant prancing horse embossed in the driveway by the 19th hole clubhouse. I was reminded of meeting Frank Hershey, designer of the Ford Thunderbird, at the Pebble Beach concours and his reminiscing of obtaining Henry Ford II's blessing to build the compact car because of its ability to carry two sets of clubs in the trunk! Dinner at the Close House was exceptional. Studying the wine list, a 2003 Chateau La-Fleur Petrus was available at £190 but I opted for the house Syrah to accompany pork loin and black pudding.

The weather didn't relent, with local news reporting that a month's rain had fallen in a day and warning of flooding. The Cortina started with a turn of the key without any choke and we soon headed along the arrow straight B6348 military road towards Housesteads Roman fort on Hadrian's Wall. Built in AD122 to secure the Roman Empire and stretching 80 miles from Newcastle to Carlisle, it took six years to build requiring a million cubic meters of stone of which a credible amount is still standing. Entry to the Fort is via a steep shale path to a strategic view to all points of the compass. One can only imagine the reaction of legioneers from the Mediterranean to this blustery location; in fact the information signs indicate Syrian archers did a tour of duty. One of the popular buildings for them I guess would have been the grain stores, whose hypercaust heating can still be seen today. Unlike so many Roman ruins in the UK, here much survives and from the north gate you can see the stone wall snaking its way over the crags.

This page: **FORD-LOTUS CORTINA MK1 1965,** driving at speed in Northumberland. Right: **FORD-LOTUS CORTINA MK1 1965,** crossing river Wasbeck, 2013 (Octane magazine).

Next we headed to Rothbury via the A6079 and B6342 and by now had discovered one of Northumberland's secrets. It's England's least populated county, a mere 62 people per square kilometre and has wonderful country roads that have long straights courtesy of the Romans and switchback dips due to the topography. The Lotus-Cortina came to life, 3500rpm was 60mph in fourth gear but the twenty-three mile drive required serious use of the gearbox to hustle the saloon along at a good pace. The drive was terrific and brought back memories of driving my Alfa Romeo Giulia Sprint in club rallies, the Italian car having a similar powertrain but with a five speed box.

At Wallington House there was a beautiful humpback bridge that crossed a swollen River Wansbeck before arriving in Rothbury to visit Cragside house, only to be faced with road closure due to flooding. Plan B was a lunch of Northumberland cheeses at the Congregational Art Gallery before a diversion to Eshott Hall. The hotel was warm and the young friendly staff showed us to the aptly named Italian room commenting that the little Lotus-Cortina must have been fun to drive.

It was an early start for the drive north to meet Mike and Beth Mills, who the National Park had asked to be our guides up College Valley in the Cheviot Hills, where only ten cars a day are permitted. Road trips have a habit of turning up the

unexpected. Mike is the owner of one of the first ever sport saloons, a 1930 Riley Alpine 6/14. This lightweight fabric bodied four door was equipped with twin camshafts, crossflow hemi cylinder head and 1600cc engine, at the time when Ford had barely ceased production of the Model T. The clouds rolled in as we climbed up the narrow road to the valley stopping at the Allied airmen memorial adjacent to Cuddystone Hall. Erected in 1995, the 50th Anniversary of VE day, it marked the location and model of aircraft whose crews had succumbed to atrocious weather or primitive navigation aids over the Cheviots. In fact we could not see through the mist and were denied a view of hills such as Sinkside and Black Haggs.

From Wooler we drove north and crossed the Scottish border, the car and driver revelling on the traffic-free sinuous roads to the market town of Duns, where there is the Jim Clark Room. This small, free museum is dedicated to the double F1 Champion of 1963/65 and the greatest Lotus-Cortina driver, the 1964 British Touring car champion. The room is like a giant trophy cabinet chronicling the sporting life of the Berwickshire farmer that some would say became our greatest racing driver. One period photograph shows the maestro freewheeling the Cortina at Brands Hatch in 1964. We stop and watch period films of Clark delicately hustling his F1 Lotus around Oulton Park. Jim Clark was famously a member of the Borders Reiver

Motor Club and we drove south back across the English border on a route that his less popular ancestors might have taken. Northumberland in the 15th Century was known as a lawless territory with groups of raiders causing the English crown to take similar measures to the Romans, which has resulted in Northumberland's many castles. Eshott Hall wasn't fortified but it was built in 1660, and that night we feasted on guinea fowl, sweet potato and baby vegetables with parsnip puree courtesy of chef Chris Wood.

Our final day's tour began with Cragside house postponed on Tuesday by the floods. This impressive Arts and Crafts house built by lawyer turned engineer William George Armstrong in 1863 is packed with innovations that might be common place today but were revolutionary at the time. Armstrong's company harnessed the power of water for projects such as the lifting gear of Tower Bridge and, at his home, water powered passenger lift. By 1881 was using electric lighting powered by hydroelectric energy from his own power station and by 1885 he was on the telephone. Cragside also sports a six mile drive through the estate, which unfortunately has a 15mph speed limit. It would have made a great rally stage for our Cortina; we had to make do with the B6341 east to the coast instead.

The steep hill out of Rothbury requires second gear and

highlights a lack of torque (107lb ft @ 4500rpm) from the 1600cc twin cam but once out on the moorland road the car came alive. The combination of Lotus suspension and Yokohama tyres coped with sweeping gravel covered bends, there was near zero body roll and only a hint of oversteer. We blasted along the straights with rollercoaster dips and never bottomed out. I could use the 110bhp all the time secure in the period standard seats.

We had an invitation for tea at Howick Hall, the ancestral home to the Grey family, where Charles, the second Earl Grey had a Chinese mandarin blend a tea to offset the lime taste of the spring water. He became Prime Minister in 1830 but failed to register the blend so the family haven't benefited. The gardens and tearooms ooze eighteenth century grandeur. Before we departed we were asked to photograph the car in front of the house for their website. It was mid afternoon before we reached the Northumberland coastal route but the light was becoming interesting and the road deserted. We could see Bamburgh castle on a rock outcrop from the Lotus as we headed north but it was not until passing through the village and out into the sand dunes did we gain the quintessential vista of beach and medieval castle. Norman in origin, the castle was the first to fall to artillery fire during a nine month siege in the Wars of the Roses. The present grand structure is the responsibility of numerous owners including Mr Armstrong.

FORD-LOTUS CORTINA MK1
1965, parked on the Causeway
to Holy Island, Northumberland,
2013 (Automobile).

The afternoon shadows were lengthening as we approached the causeway to Holy Island. Checking the tide tables, we had just two hours to cross to the island to savour the Lindisfarne Priory and Castle. At the car park there are red signs warning of dire consequences of attempting to cross to the mainland in the red tide time zone! The monastic ruins and a bracing walk around the small harbour, where the local fishermen had come up with a novel way of recycling old boats into huts by turning them upside-down, took longer than planned so we headed back across the bay towards our last night in Berwick-upon-Tweed.

The Northumbrian Guest House is a located within the town walls and like much of the town, is Georgian. Berwick changed hands between Scotland and England in the medieval times but it was Elizabeth I who equipped it with state of the art defensive walls and the town's architecture has a Scandinavian feel. Ian Kille, our host, pointed us in the right direction to take in as much of the town as possible before sunset. The bridges over the Tweed include George Stephenson's Royal Boarder Bridge, which dominates. It was built in 1847 and its 28 arches carry the east coast mainline.

The 950-mile drive to Northumberland in the Lotus-Cortina proved hugely rewarding. The county has dramatic topography, a wealth of historic sites, great hotels and friendly chatty people. We will return.

ASTON MARTIN DB5 1963,
James Bond Aston Martin DB5
on display in The Royal Automobile Club Pall Mall, London,
2012 (Royal Automobile Club).

ROYAL AUTOMOBILE CLUB

The attractive blonde commented to her partner while exiting the lift, "I'm sure that that racing car wasn't there when we came back to the club last night." True, the Red Bull Racing F1 car wasn't there; it had been expertly manoeuvred up ramps through rotating doors and squeezed between stone pillars at dawn that morning by Tony Worsfold and his team, to be displayed in the rotunda of the Royal Automobile Club in Pall Mall.

"Displaying cars in the RAC Club goes back to the 1960s when the Aston Martin James Bond DB5 was shown," said Ben Cussons of the motoring committee and prime selector of the rolling exhibits. "People love to see the automobiles as this is a motoring club." My connection to the show has been to photograph the cars on display, in this, the centenary year of 'the Palace of Pall Mall'. The cars that are displayed are of historical significance, technically advanced or promoting an event that might be taking place at the vast Edwardian building designed by Mewes & Davis. George Kennedy, a past Secretary of the RAC, decreed that the Rotunda was not to be any old car showroom, hence the cars recently shown include Sir Henry Segrave's 1924 Sunbeam, the Mars Rover vehicle, Peugeot 908 Le Mans winning car, Racing Green SR Zero, Gordon Murray T27 and Tim Birkin's blower Bentley to list a few.

To photograph the automobiles entering the Club I forced myself out of bed at 4.30am to make the scooter ride through deserted London streets to watch how the vast red vintage racing Bentley made its entry into the building. First the rotating

doors had to be removed and then an aluminium ramp was constructed, which was first used in 2005 to allow a Rolls-Royce Phantom entry, as previous ramps had not been able to take the weight of Goodwood's finest. In the Birkin Bentley's case, an electric winch was attached and after much lining up and sighting, Tony Worsfold gave the all clear to start the sedate climb up to nine feet from street level. The porter at the concierge desk, sorting the newspapers for guests, didn't even look up as the vintage racing car passed. After the Bentley had been parked on the blue and gold carpet, a process that took about 5 minutes, Tony commented that the car had been a tight fit between the staircase pillars but was a piece of cake compared with the Ford Galaxy 500 American muscle car, which required gently leaning on the side panels to gain entry!

I photograph the cars at various times of the day and noticed, especially when looking down from the balcony above members, guests and staff peering into the cars, some stand and read the information boards. Others I can hear comment on how they have owned similar cars and waiters would stop carrying a tray of drinks to snatch a quick look at Sebastian Vettel's Red Bull F1 car. Early one morning Sir Paul Smith, fashion designer, so impressed by the 1927 Duesenberg X Type, photographed the car in the rotunda and sent a set of photographs complementing owner Peter Heydon on such a wonderful automobile. Placing a car in such a surreal location is very British but for a motoring club it provides a topic for debate and comment for members and their guests en route to the dining room!

FIAT S76-TIPO12, 1911.

FERRARI 250 GTO, 1962.

FERRARI 250 GT SWB, 1961.

LAMBORGHINI MIRA P400, 1968.

ROLLS-ROYCE SILVER GHOST, 1908.

FERRARI 290MM, 1956.

MERCEDES-BENZ. F1 W05 HYBRID, 2014.

FERRARI F40, 1990.

TALBOT-LAGO T26 GRAND SPORT, 1950.

PORSCHE 917, 1970.

ALFA ROMEO 8C2300, 1932.

AUDI R18 E-TRON, 2013.

PORSCHE 956, 1983.

NISSAN DELTA WING, 2012.

FERRARI 340/375MM, 1953.

ASTON MARTIN DB3S, 1954.

TOURING DISCO VOLANTE, 2014.

PAGANI ZONDA S ROADSTER, 2005.

SIR PAUL SMITH MINI, 1998.

ALFA ROMEO SZ, 1961.

CITROEN SM, 1972.

FORD GT, 2015.

LANCIA DELTA S4, 1986.

FERRARI 166MM, 1950.

Top, from left:
NIKKOMAT FTN, 1972.
NIKON FM2, 1977.
HASSELBLAD 500CM, 1974.
NIKON F4, 1988.

Bottom, from left:
WISTA TECHNICAL CAMERA 5X4, 1999.
CANON EOS 5D, 2012.
LUMIX GF-1, 2009.
LUMIX GX 8, 2015.

PHOTO NOTES

Since graduating from college in 1974, the only photographic process that remains consistent today is that light passes through the lens of the camera. Indeed the cameras have changed beyond all recognition since I was given a Nikkormat FTN for my 21st birthday. The single lens reflex used 35mm film and had totally mechanical functions, including the built-in light meter, lens focusing and film advance.

This was to be the first of a string of Nikon products. I loved the way the camera system was easy to use under pressure, with great lens quality and tough construction that stood up to the knocks and bad weather conditions I worked in on location. I moved on to FM2 and FE versions of the Japanese company's compact camera bodies and then purchased a Nikon F3, which was to become the real workhorse for location shoots. In 1976 I needed a medium format camera for my growing studio music business assignments. I bought a second-hand Hasselblad 500CM, the Rolls-Royce of cameras with two lenses, 50 and 80mm, and a magical Polaroid back, which made previewing a set up possible. I still own this camera, which I used for most of the album covers and occasional car sessions up to 2005.

In the early 90s yet another technical innovation made my life easier; auto focus. It was then that I abandoned Nikon and purchased a range of Canon EOS cameras and lenses. The company's ultrasonic motors were fast and silent and made the opposition's system sound and work like a medieval siege engine.

The system had served me well so when I decided to move totally to the digital platform I went for the full frame EOS 1DS, with five memory cards. I could have bought a good Ford Focus for the nearly six thousand pounds I paid for the kit. Price aside it was a great camera and made the change over from film simple.

The march of change continues to a point where I now use Lumix Micro four-thirds camera systems. These mirrorless gems are small, light and quick to use. They are so much fun that I probably use them too much. Other members of my profession scorn them as lacking in photographers presence, whatever that is.

Over my career I have worked with a wide range of camera, lighting and indeed computer software but though important to me they are just a means of producing the best possible images. Recently I was in Yosemite National Park in California and came upon a keen group of amateur photographers; to a man and a woman all had far more sophisticated and expensive cameras on their tripods than my beat-up Lumix!

CREDITS

Beverley Ballard picture editor of FAB 208 magazine in 1974.

Wendy Harrop art director of Car magazine in 1976.

David E Davis Jr. editor in Chief of Car & Driver in 1983.

All the writers, editors, bands, managers and PRs that I have had the pleasure to work with.

Nick Mason for writing nice things in his introduction.

Sir Paul Smith for his design thoughts.

Bill Smith for remembering 1970s photo sessions.

Mike Pickles of the Really Useful Products Ltd whose enthusiasm for the project has been invaluable.

Michael Floyd editor of Automobile magazine and Jean Jennings for permission to publish 'Monterey or Bust' road trip.

Greg Fountain editor of Car magazine for permission to publish Car Photo copy.

David Lillywhite editor of Octane magazine for his help in editing.

Dale Drinnon writer of 'Key to the Highway' story.

Peter Foubister Motoring Secretary of the Royal Automobile Club for permission to use the Rotunda cars images.

Jacquie Tilley and the team Katy & Jade at Tilley Associates for their hard work and design excellence in the production of this book.

Rachel Donnelly, Mike Pickles' PA. For dealing with all the business stuff.

Matt Booker and Cousin for their help with all things print.

Shea Kelly of Pavement for his pre-press expertise.